陇东学院学科建设经费资助
陇东学院学术著作基金资助出版
甘肃省教育厅高校教师创新基金项目 2024B-167

翻译规范背景下《儒林外史》英译本翻译风格研究
——语料库驱动的研究范式

A Corpus-Driven Study of Translation Style in the English Version of *Ru Lin Wai Shi* Under the Context of Translation Norms

黄景芸 著

吉林大学出版社
·长春·

图书在版编目(CIP)数据

翻译规范背景下《儒林外史》英译本翻译风格研究 ：语料库驱动的研究范式 = A Corpus-Driven Study of Translation Style in the English Version of Ru Lin Wai Shi Under the Context of Translation Norms ：英文 / 黄景芸著. — 长春 ： 吉林大学出版社， 2024.5
ISBN 978-7-5768-3153-5

Ⅰ. ①翻… Ⅱ. ①黄… Ⅲ. ①《儒林外史》—英语—文学翻译—研究 Ⅳ. ① H315.9 ② I207.419

中国国家版本馆 CIP 数据核字 (2024) 第 087262 号

书　　名：翻译规范背景下《儒林外史》英译本翻译风格研究：
　　　　　语料库驱动的研究范式
　　　　　FANYI GUIFAN BEIJING XIA《RULIN WAISHI》YINGYI BEN FANYI
　　　　　FENGGE YANJIU:YULIAOKU QUDONG DE YANJIU FANSHI

作　　者：黄景芸
策划编辑：邵宇彤
责任编辑：高珊珊
责任校对：郭湘怡
装帧设计：寒　露
出版发行：吉林大学出版社
社　　址：长春市人民大街 4059 号
邮政编码：130021
发行电话：0431-89580036/58
网　　址：http://www.jlup.com.cn
电子邮箱：jldxcbs@sina.com
印　　刷：河北万卷印刷有限公司
成品尺寸：170mm×240mm　　16 开
印　　张：11.75
字　　数：205 千字
版　　次：2024 年 5 月第 1 版
印　　次：2024 年 5 月第 1 次
书　　号：ISBN 978-7-5768-3153-5
定　　价：68.00 元

Preface

Ru Lin Wai Shi (*The Scholars*), penned by Wu Jingzi, a distinguished novelist of the Qing Dynasty, is a masterpiece in the realm of Chinese classical literature. Characterized by its satirical approach in critiquing the societal errors of its time, this novel occupies a distinct place in the annals of Chinese literary history. Despite the significant research value inherent in the original text, the scholarly engagement with its English translation is disproportionately sparse, both in terms of quality and quantity, failing to match the original's elevated status in Chinese literature. This dissertation aims to address this disparity by concentrating on three critical areas where existing research is deficient: the absence of multidimensional analytical perspectives, the lack of systematic empirical support, and a general oversight regarding the intricacies of translation norms.

This research is underpinned by Jürgen Habermas's theory of communicative action, which provides a robust theoretical framework for examining the translation norms of *The Scholars*. Through a meticulously constructed corpus, this study delves into the linguistic features of the English translation by the Yangs. Drawing upon Hu Xianyao's revised definition and categorization of translation norms, the dissertation investigates the alignment between linguistic elements and operational norms. This includes exploring dimensions such as explicitness versus implicitness, and the dichotomy of simplification versus complication, alongside parataxis versus hypotaxis, and the contrasts between normalization and deviation.

The methodology employed in this research is twofold. Firstly, a comparative corpus analysis is conducted using Joseph Heller's *Catch-22*, which shares similarities with *The Scholars* in genre, token, and the time span of the original text. This comparison serves to contextualize the translation within a broader literary framework. Secondly, a parallel corpus is constructed from a random selection of 42 chapters of *The Scholars*, with a specific focus on marking parts of speech, idioms, and religious terms. This detailed analysis enables a nuanced understanding of the translation strategies employed.

The corpus analysis yields several key findings. It reveals a tendency towards simplification in the English translation of *The Scholars*, especially in terms of word usage compared to the source text. There is a notable decrease in the use of nouns, particularly proper names, and an increased reliance on pronouns. This linguistic shift points to a broader trend in the translation norms adopted. Additionally, the study identifies a significant increase in the use of prepositions and conjunctions, indicating a move towards greater explicitness in the translation. In terms of syntactic structure, the English version is characterized by shorter sentence lengths and a more pronounced inclination towards hypotaxis, compared to the source text.

These findings have profound implications for understanding the translation of *The Scholars*. They highlight the dominant role of normalization norms, with deviation playing a secondary but significant role. When analyzing the cultural context of the English translation of *The Scholars*, we discovered that the translation norms reflected not only the social and cultural background of that era but also demonstrated the influence of the translator's personal experience and poetic traditions on the translation style of this version. By addressing the research gaps in the study of *The Scholars*' translation, this dissertation contributes to a deeper comprehension of the social aspects of literary translation, shedding light on the cultural and linguistic dynamics that govern the process.

In conclusion, this study not only enriches the academic discourse on translation norms but also underscores the practical significance of this research approach. By applying and validating the methodology of translation norm study, it offers valuable insights into the translation process, enhancing our understanding of the English version of *The Scholars* and affirming its rightful place in the literary canon.

前言

《儒林外史》，清代著名作家吴敬梓之杰作，不仅在中国古典小说中占有重要地位，更以其独到的批判时代弊端的讽刺手法，在中国文学史上独树一帜。然而，尽管原著研究价值非凡，其英文译本的研究在数量和质量上却与原著的重要地位不相匹配。现有研究普遍存在三大不足：缺乏多维度分析、缺少系统的实证支持、忽视翻译规范的复杂性。

本研究立足尤尔根·哈贝马斯（Habermas）的交际行为理论，旨在通过对杨宪益夫妇英译本语言特征的深入剖析，重构《儒林外史》的翻译规范。研究基于胡显耀对翻译规范的新定义及分类，着重考察语言特征与操作规范（如明确性与含蓄性、简化与复杂化、并列与从属、规范化与偏离等）间的相互关系。

研究方法包括两个部分：首先，通过与《第二十二条军规》（在形符数、语域以及出版时间上与《儒林外史》相似）的比较，建立了一个类比语料库。其次，通过对《儒林外史》42 章的随机抽样，标记词性、成语和宗教术语，构建平行语料库。分析发现，与原文相比，英文版在词汇使用上趋向简化，代词使用更频繁，尤其是名词，特别是人名的使用频率显著降低。此外，英文译本在句法结构上平均句长更短，偏向复杂结构，体现在介词和连词的使用频率明显增加。

这些发现揭示了《儒林外史》英文版在传统化期待规范与陌生化期待规范方面同时作用的特点，其中传统化期待规范占主导地位。此外，在分析《儒林外史》英译本的文化语境时，我们发现其所反映的翻译规范不仅揭示了当时的社会文化背景，还体现了译者的个人经历和诗学传统对此译本翻译风格的影响。本研究填补了《儒林外史》翻译规范研究的空白，有助于深化对文学翻译社会层面的理解，揭示文化和语言动态对翻译过程的影响。

综上所述，本研究不仅丰富了翻译规范的学术讨论，而且强调了此类研究方法的实践意义。通过应用和验证翻译规范研究的方法论，本研究提供了对翻译过程的深入见解，增强了我们对《儒林外史》英文版的理解，并确认了其在文学典藏中的合理存在。

Contents

Chapter One

Introduction

1.1 Research Background

Ru Lin Wai Shi (*The Scholars* in English version), authored by Wu Jingzi, a prominent novelist of the Qing Dynasty, stands as a monumental work in the realm of Chinese classical literature. Its unique blend of satire and introspection has earned it a place alongside *A Dream of Red Mansions* as one of the twin jewels of Chinese literary tradition. The novel's structure, described by Lu Xun as "a lengthy novel but similar to short stories" (Lu Xun, 2009:154), and its art of irony, aimed at "castigating the errors of the times out of unselfish motives" (ibid:155), deftly unveil the material and spiritual poverty of feudal scholars, offering a profound critique of traditional bachelor culture.

Ru Lin Wai Shi' significant place in Chinese literature is unquestionable, and its value extends well beyond China's borders. In countries like the UK, France, Germany, Russia, and Japan, translated versions of the novel have been highly acclaimed (Chen Li, 2009:36). Despite the original text's rich research potential and its longstanding global popularity, studies on its English version, both in quantity and quality, have struggled to match the stature of this classic work. As of January 2024, CNKI lists 60 articles focusing on the English translation of *The Scholars*. These studies have approached the translation from various angles, including translator subjectivity, cultural, linguistic, and communicative aspects, and translation strategies. However, there remains a significant gap in the depth and breadth of this research.

One notable shortcoming is the lack of multidimensional perspectives. Most existing research tends to focus on single theoretical frameworks, like Skopos theory, relevance theory, hermeneutics, and multiculturalism, rarely combining diverse viewpoints and methodologies. Furthermore, there is a notable lack of statistical and systematic empirical support. Among the existing studies, only a handful, such as those by Cong Qianqian(2011), who examined marked passive sentences, and Wang Yingjun(2014), who explored the English translation of Chinese humorous texts with a case study of *Ru Lin Wai Shi* and its English version, have employed parallel corpus methodology. Zeng Qi's(2002) work, which used quantitative methods to analyze translation strategies of culture-loaded words and common sayings in *Ru Lin Wai Shi*, is another rare example.

Moreover, there has been insufficient attention to the complexity and variability of translation norms. This study aims to address these gaps by employing corpus linguistics to clearly define the operational norms that influence translators' decisions regarding translation strategies. This approach allows for a detailed analysis of translation choices and the underlying factors influencing these decisions. The study will also explore the social and cultural contexts influencing the formation of these norms.

The Scholars presents a fascinating case for study due to its historical and cultural significance. The novel, written during a time of immense social change in China, offers insight into the shifting attitudes and values of the period. The English translation, therefore, is not just a linguistic transfer but a cultural bridge, carrying with it the nuances of a time long past. This study will delve into how the translator navigates the complex interplay of retaining the novel's original flavor while making it accessible and engaging for an English-speaking audience.

In addition to a literary analysis, this research will also encompass a broader sociolinguistic perspective. It will examine how *The Scholars* reflects and responds to the socio-political context of both the source and target cultures. By doing so, the research will contribute to a more comprehensive understanding of cross-cultural literary exchange and the role of translation in shaping global perceptions of a literary work.

Lastly, this research will contribute to the field of translation studies by offering a nuanced view of the decision-making process in literary translation. By analyzing specific examples from the English version of *The Scholars*, the study will provide insights into how translators navigate linguistic challenges, cultural differences, and the expectations of a diverse readership. The findings will not only shed light on the particular case of *The Scholars* but also offer broader implications for the translation of other literary works.

In conclusion, this research aims to provide a comprehensive analysis of the English translation of *Ru Lin Wai Shi*, exploring the interplay of linguistic, cultural, and social factors. By doing so, it seeks to contribute to a deeper understanding of the intricacies involved in translating a culturally rich and historically significant literary work.

1.2 Research Aim and Method

Research Purpose

The primary objective of this thesis is to delineate and analyze the translation norms in the English version of *Ru Lin Wai Shi* (*The Scholars*), following the convention/foreignness expectancy framework proposed by scholars in the field. This study aims to examine the translation norms at both the conventional and foreign levels within the translated text, assessing the extent to which each is achieved. Additionally, it seeks to investigate the formative factors behind these norms.

Methodological Approach

This research utilizes corpus linguistics within the framework of descriptive translation studies, employing a multi-step approach to analyze the English translation of *Ru Lin Wai Shi*. The methodology is divided into three primary stages:

Establishment of *The Scholars* Translation Corpus: The initial step involves compiling a comprehensive corpus for *The Scholars*. Multiple sources and methods, including scanning, manual input, and Internet downloads, are employed to gather materials. To expedite the process, the research primarily relies on online purchase for the raw text. Subsequently, tools such as CorpusWordParser are utilized for Chinese word segmentation and POS tagging, while TreeTagger for Windows 3.0 is employed for English POS tagging. The Tmxmall tool is used to align the original text and its translation at the sentence level. In addition to the parallel corpus, a comparative corpus is developed using the novel *Catch-22*, which shares similarities in genre, token, and time span with *The Scholars*.

Research Process of Translation Norms: Following the methodology of Hu Xianyao (2006), this thesis examines translation norms through both external and internal lenses. The process involves three stages: (a) hypothesizing operational norms; (b) examining corpus data; and (c) analyzing expectation norms. This methodology enables a comprehensive exploration of translation norms, from practical operations to the broader expectations they reflect.

Analysis of Underlying Factors in Translation Norms: The third stage involves a deep analysis of the reasons behind the translation norms. By studying the translated language features, the research aims to understand the constraints influencing translation behavior and to identify both the norms themselves and the social-cultural factors underpinning them.

Qualitative and Quantitative Analysis

Acknowledging the importance of a holistic approach, this study incorporates both qualitative and quantitative methods to systematically validate the translation norms. Whereas prior research often focused on individual judgment through limited examples, this study broadens the scope by:

Qualitative Analysis: A detailed examination of specific instances within the translation to explore the translator's decisions in handling cultural references, idiomatic expressions, and style. This analysis aims to understand how the translation mediates between the original Chinese context and the target English audience.

Quantitative Analysis: Statistical analysis of linguistic patterns, frequency of linguistic features, and syntactic structures. This method identifies trends in the translation, providing empirical support to the qualitative insights.

In-Depth Exploration of Translation Norms

The study delves into various aspects of translation norms:

Operational Norms: Analyzing practical translation choices, such as vocabulary, syntax, and structure, to understand the operational decisions and strategies employed by the translator.

Expectation Norms: Investigating the translation's alignment with or divergence from the norms expected by the target language audience.

Contribution to Descriptive Translation Studies and Corpus Linguistics

Rooted in descriptive translation studies and corpus linguistics, this research aims to contribute significantly to both fields. By offering comprehensive analyses that combine qualitative insights with quantitative data, the study sheds light on the complexity of translating a culturally rich text like *The Scholars*. It aims to provide nuanced understanding of translation norms, elucidating the translator's strategies in navigating linguistic and cultural differences.

Expected Outcomes and Implications

The research is expected to yield:

Detailed understanding of the translation norms in *The Scholars*.

Insights into the balance between conventionality and foreignness in translation.

A deeper comprehension of how socio-cultural factors influence translation choices.

Contributions to translation studies methodology, particularly in applying corpus linguistics to literary translations.

In sum, this thesis endeavors to bridge existing research gaps in the study of *The Scholars* through a corpus-driven approach that integrates both qualitative and quantitative analyses. The findings aim to enhance our understanding of translation norms and contribute to the broader field of translation studies, particularly in the context of Chinese to English literary translation.

1.3 Organization of the Study

This thesis, comprising six meticulously structured chapters, offers an in-depth exploration of the translation norms in the English version of *Ru Lin Wai Shi* (*The Scholars*). Each chapter is designed to build upon the previous one, methodically unfolding the research in a coherent and comprehensive manner.

Chapter One: Introduction

The introductory chapter sets the stage for the entire study. It begins by elucidating the rationale behind choosing *The Scholars* for this research, highlighting its significance in the realm of translation studies. This chapter outlines the main aims of the thesis, detailing the objectives that the research intends to achieve. It also delves into the methodologies employed, offering a preview of the analytical tools and techniques used in the study. Furthermore, the content of the study is summarized, providing a snapshot of what each subsequent chapter entails. Lastly, this chapter underscores the significance of the research, discussing its expected contributions to the field of translation studies and its relevance in the broader context of literary analysis.

Chapter Two: Literature Review

Chapter Two presents a comprehensive review of existing literature. It bifurcates the review into two main sections: first, an examination of previous studies on *Ru Lin Wai Shi* and its English translation *The Scholars*, and second, an exploration of research concerning translation norms. By doing so, the chapter identifies the gaps in current scholarship, setting the foundation for the research questions and hypotheses of this thesis. This literature review not only contextualizes the study within the existing body of work but also justifies the need for further exploration in this area.

Chapter Three: Theoretical Framework

The third chapter is pivotal as it introduces the theoretical framework underpinning the study. It begins by defining key concepts and terminologies relevant to the research, ensuring clarity and precision in the subsequent analysis. The chapter then proceeds to discuss the classification of translation norms, elaborating on how these norms have been conceptualized and categorized in previous studies. This theoretical grounding is crucial for the analysis carried out in later chapters, as it provides the lens through which the data is interpreted.

Chapter Four: Research Methodology

Chapter Four is dedicated to the research methodology of the study. It elaborates on the specific research questions that guide the investigation and details the methodological approach adopted to address these questions. The chapter introduces the major research instruments used, such as AntConc and PowerGREP 4, and explains their relevance and functionality in the context of this research. Furthermore, it outlines the procedures for data collection and analysis, providing a clear roadmap of how the research is conducted. This chapter ensures transparency and replicability in the research process, which are vital for academic rigor.

Chapter Five: Translation Norms in *The Scholars*

The fifth chapter is where the theoretical framework and methodologies converge in the application. It meticulously describes various characteristics, from lexical categories to syntax, to ascertain the translation norms in *The Scholars*. This chapter is the core of the thesis, where the collected data is analyzed, and findings are drawn. It involves a detailed discussion of the results, linking them back to the research questions and theoretical framework. The analysis is presented in a logical and coherent manner, with each finding substantiated by evidence from the data.

Chapter Six: Conclusion

The final chapter serves as the conclusion of the thesis. It summarizes the major findings of the study, highlighting how the research contributes to the existing knowledge on translation norms in *The Scholars*. This chapter also discusses the implications of these findings, both for the field of translation studies and for the understanding of *The Scholars* as a literary work. Moreover, it acknowledges the limitations of the study, suggesting areas for future research. This chapter not only wraps up the study but also opens avenues for further scholarly inquiry.

Extended Discussion

In addition to the main content, each chapter delves into subtler aspects of the study. The introduction, for instance, discusses the historical and cultural significance of *The Scholars* and its impact on Chinese literature. The literature review not only identifies gaps but also critically analyzes the methodologies and findings of previous research, providing a thorough background for the study.

The theoretical framework chapter discusses various theories of translation and their applicability to *The Scholars*, while the methodology chapter gives an in-depth explanation of the corpus linguistic approach and its relevance in translation studies. The data analysis chapter not only presents findings but also engages in a critical discussion of these results, comparing them with existing literature and theories.

Lastly, the conclusion synthesizes all the chapters, providing a holistic view of the research and its contributions to the field. It also proposes how these findings can be applied in practical translation scenarios, thus bridging the gap between academic research and real-world application.

Chapter Two

Literature Review

Since the dawn of the 20th century, *The Scholars*, a seminal work in the annals of Chinese literature, has seen multiple translations across various languages including English, French, German, Russian, and Japanese. This widespread translation reflects the novel's global appeal and the intrigue it holds in understanding Chinese culture and literature. Chinese scholars like Ge Chuangui, Xu Zhenping, Wang Jizhen, Zhang Xincang, among others, have contributed to its translation, albeit in parts. The complete translation of *Ru Lin Wai Shi* by Yang Hsien-yi and his wife Gladys Yang stands as a significant accomplishment, having been included in the prestigious Library of Chinese Classics. This particular translation is notable not only for its comprehensiveness but also for the depth and nuance it brings to a complex cultural narrative.

The cultural richness and the inherent complexity in translating *Ru Lin Wai Shi* make it a subject of diverse and extensive study. The novel's intricate portrayal of Chinese society and its idiomatic language pose considerable challenges to translators, necessitating a careful balance between cultural fidelity and linguistic fluidity. This complexity has resulted in a variety of research approaches and perspectives, each contributing to a deeper understanding of the novel and its translation.

This chapter aims to accomplish two primary objectives. Firstly, it will synthesize the existing research on *The Scholars*, drawing from a multitude of perspectives to outline the current research landscape. This synthesis will not only highlight the unique characteristics of the research conducted on this novel but also identify gaps and shortcomings in the existing studies.

The review will delve into how different scholars have approached the text, analyzing their methodologies, findings, and the contributions they have made to the understanding of the novel and its translations.

Secondly, the chapter will provide a critical overview of the development of translation norms as a concept and practice. It will explore how the theory and application of translation norms have evolved over time, examining the achievements and limitations of these conceptual and methodological developments.

2.1 Previous Researches on *Ru Lin Wai Shi*

Previous Researches on *Ru Lin Wai Shi*

Over the past 72 years, from 1952 to 2024, as we can see in Figure 2.1, *Ru Lin Wai Shi* has been a focal point of academic inquiry, as evidenced by the 2,605 articles identified in CNKI (China National Knowledge Infrastructure) that use it as a keyword. These works encompass a wide range of journal articles and dissertations, indicating the novel's significant impact on literary and cultural studies.

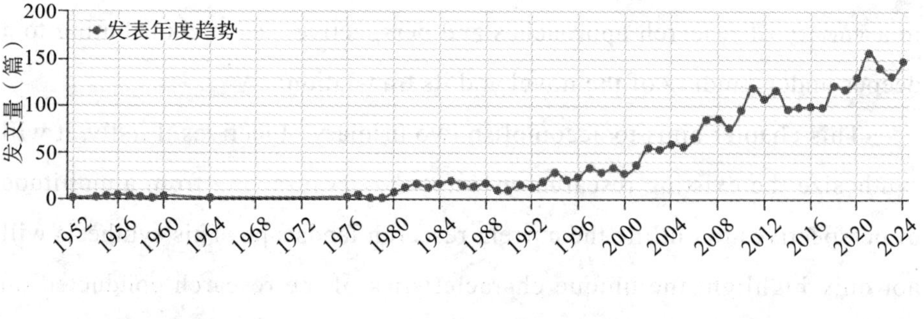

Figure 2.1 The Tendency of Studying *Ru Lin Wai Shi*

Early Research Trends (1952—1992)

In the initial forty years, from 1952 to 1992, academic engagement with *Ru Lin Wai Shi* was relatively modest, with no more than 40 research papers published annually. During this period, the focus was primarily on the novel's literary analysis, cultural significance, and its role in the context of Chinese classical literature. Studies often centered on thematic exploration, character analysis, and the novel's stylistic features. Researchers were beginning to recognize the novel's intricate portrayal of Qing Dynasty society and its satirical undertones.

Growing Interest and Diversification (1993—2024)

The year 1996 marked a significant turning point in the research trend of *Ru Lin Wai Shi*. There was a notable increase in scholarly interest, which led to a diversification of research themes and methodologies. This period saw an expansion beyond traditional literary analysis to include perspectives from history, sociology, and cultural studies.

Historical and Sociological Approaches: Researchers began to explore the novel's historical accuracy and its reflection of social dynamics during the Qing Dynasty. Studies examined the social critique implicit in Wu Jingzi's narrative, offering insights into the author's commentary on the societal norms and practices of his time.

Cultural Analysis: Researchers delved deeper into the cultural implications of the novel. Studies focused on understanding the portrayal of traditional Chinese values, Confucian ideals, and the critique of the feudal system present in the narrative.

Critical Reception and Influence: The later years also witnessed an increased focus on the novel's critical reception and its influence on both Chinese and global literature. The impact of *Ru Lin Wai Shi* on subsequent literary works and its role in shaping perceptions of Chinese culture were key areas of exploration.

Breakthroughs and Innovations

The surge in research led to significant breakthroughs, particularly in understanding the novel's multifaceted nature. Innovative approaches, including digital humanities and corpus linguistics, began to be applied, allowing for more sophisticated textual analysis and interpretation. The utilization of these modern methodologies facilitated a more nuanced understanding of Wu Jingzi's narrative techniques and thematic complexity.

The evolving research trajectory of *Ru Lin Wai Shi* reflects its enduring relevance and the rich, diverse avenues of inquiry it offers. From its early days of modest academic attention to its current status as a subject of extensive, multidisciplinary study, *Ru Lin Wai Shi* continues to be a valuable resource for understanding Chinese literature and culture.

2.2 Previous Researches on the English Version of *Ru Lin Wai Shi*

The Scholars, translated by Yang Hsien-yi and his wife Gladys Yang, holds the distinction of being the only complete English translation of *Ru Lin Wai Shi*. This translation has become a focal point for scholars and translators, sparking a wide range of academic inquiries. By January 2024, CNKI lists 60 articles specifically focusing on this English version, indicating significant scholarly interest. Furthermore, Figure 2.2, depicting the comparison between studies in "Chinese Literature" and those in "Foreign Language", reveals the discrepancy in research intensity between the original and the translated text.

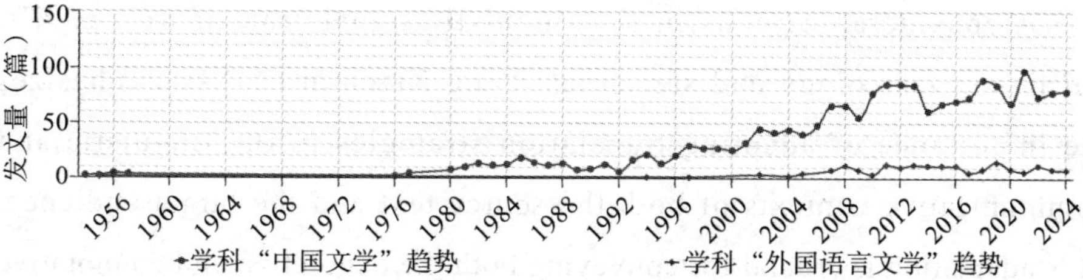

Figure 2.2 The Research Tendency in *Ru Lin Wai Shi* and *The Scholars*

Despite *The Scholars* being a monumental work in Chinese literature, the research on its English translation appears to have attracted less attention, especially within the domestic translation community. This gap is intriguing, given the translation's importance in bridging cultural and linguistic divides.

A thorough review of the existing literature reveals that the research on the English version of *The Scholars* can be broadly classified into five distinct perspectives: linguistics, culture, translator, translation strategies, and others. Each category offers unique insights and contributes to a fuller understanding of the translation's complexity and nuances.

2.2.1 Perspective of Linguistic

The translation of Chinese classical literature, especially works like *The Scholars*, presents unique challenges and opportunities from a linguistic perspective. This literature review delves into various studies that explore these challenges, focusing on how translators overcome linguistic barriers to effectively convey the rich tapestry of Chinese culture, history, and societal norms to a global audience.

Lexicology and Semantics

A considerable focus in the linguistic translation of *Ru Lin Wai Shi* lies in lexicology and semantics. Peng Xiaomin (2014) emphasizes the importance of adapting translation strategies to the linguistic and communicative contexts of both the source text and the target audience. This adaptation is crucial for conveying both the denotative and connotative meanings of culture-loaded words. Liu Yu (2014) extends this idea by applying modern prototypical categorization theory to the translation of lexical categories, offering a nuanced understanding of how categorization in one language can inform effective translation strategies in another.

Pragmatics and Syntax

The pragmatics and syntax of translation are also critical. Here, researchers explore how the grammatical and structural aspects of language influence the conveyance of meaning. This involves examining sentence structure, idiomatic expressions, and the stylistic nuances that are inherent to *The Scholars*. Feng Jie (2016)'s study is particularly insightful in this regard, employing a relevance-theoretical account to investigate the translation strategies of idioms used by the Yangs. This approach underscores the importance of relevance theory in guiding the translation process, especially in maintaining the integrity and peculiarity of idioms.

Systemic Functional Grammar and Cognitive Linguistics

Moving beyond traditional linguistic approaches, some researchers have incorporated systemic functional grammar and cognitive linguistics into their analysis. This perspective allows for a more holistic understanding of the text, considering not only the grammatical structure but also how language functions within its cultural context. Studies in this area have focused on various linguistic elements, such as words, sentences, appellations, rhetoric, and culture-loaded words, assessing how these elements interact to create meaning and how they can be effectively translated.

2.2.2 Perspectives of Translation Strategy

The translation of *The Scholars* has been a fertile ground for exploring various translation strategies. This literature review expands on the existing research, highlighting the diverse methods employed in translating this seminal Chinese work into other languages, with a particular focus on the English translations.

Semantic and Communicative Translation

Guo Xiaohui (2010) leverages Peter Newmark's semantic and communicative translation theories to analyze the translation of official titles in *The Scholars*. He advocates for a dialectical employment of both strategies, suggesting that while semantic translation should be the primary approach for official titles, communicative translation becomes crucial when the full conveyance of Chinese cultural information is at stake. This dual approach underscores the complexity of translating culturally nuanced terms.

Cultural Translation Approach

Chen Li (2008) delves into the cultural aspects of translating *Ru Lin Wai Shi*, covering areas such as ecology, linguistic culture, social culture, religious culture, and material culture. Chen advocates for a predominance of foreignization in translating Chinese literary works into English, emphasizing the importance of preserving cultural identity in the translation process. This approach is pivotal in maintaining the integrity of the source culture in the target language.

Verbal Humor and Bilingual Analysis

Wang Yingjun (2014) examines the unique challenge of translating verbal humor in *The Scholars*. By utilizing a systematic analysis of both the original and the English version, along with a Chinese-English bilingual parallel database, Wang provides new insights into the translation methods of humor. This study highlights the subtleties involved in translating humor, which often relies heavily on cultural and linguistic contexts.

Translation of Culture-Loaded Words

Zeng Qi (2002) conducts a statistical and theoretical analysis of the translation methods of culture-loaded words and expressions in *The Scholars*. Zeng concludes that these strategies are intricately linked to the purpose of translation, the similarities and differences between source and target cultures, the translator's attitude towards both cultures, and their anticipation of the target readers' cultural background and acceptability. This study underscores the complex interplay between culture and language in translation.

Hybrid Characteristics and Functional Equivalence

Ding Shuifang and Ding Jianhai (2013) discuss the hybrid linguistic characteristics in *The Scholars*. Their approach takes into account the mixed linguistic and cultural elements that characterize the novel. By applying Nida's functional equivalence theory, they explore how the translation can achieve an equivalent effect in the target language while retaining the novel's unique cultural essence.

Descriptive Language of Mad Figures

Huang Siyi (2015) employs Foucault's madness concept to investigate the translation methods of descriptive language regarding the speeches and behaviors of mad characters in *The Scholars* and its English translation. This study is particularly insightful as it intersects linguistic analysis with philosophical concepts, illustrating how the translation of complex characters can be informed by broader theoretical frameworks.

Gap in Translation Methodology

Despite the extensive research on translation strategies, there remains a gap in the specific methodologies for translating particular language phenomena in *The Scholars*. Most studies have focused on broader strategies without delving into the intricacies of translating specific linguistic or cultural elements.

The Need for Specific Translation Laws

The existing literature indicates a need for more detailed guidelines or laws to navigate the complex task of translating specific linguistic phenomena found in *The Scholars*. This could involve more granular analysis of syntax, idiomatic expressions, or rhetorical devices unique to the source text and how they can be effectively rendered in different target languages.

Integrating Cross-Disciplinary Approaches

Future research could benefit from integrating cross-disciplinary approaches, combining linguistic, cultural, and literary analysis. This would enhance the understanding of how different translation strategies can be applied to specific language phenomena within *The Scholars*, considering not only the linguistic aspects but also the cultural and literary contexts.

Computational Linguistics and Translation Memory Software

The use of computational linguistics and translation memory software presents an exciting frontier for research in translation strategies. These technologies could offer new ways to approach the translation of classical texts like *The Scholars*, potentially streamlining the process and ensuring consistency across translations.

The translation of *The Scholars* represents a rich field of study for translation strategies. From semantic and communicative translation to the cultural translation approach, and from the translation of humor to the intricate rendering of culture-loaded words, researchers have contributed significantly to our understanding of this process. However, there is still much to explore, particularly regarding specific translation methodologies and the integration of technological tools in the translation process. Future research in this area promises to deepen our understanding of the complexity involved in translating this cornerstone of Chinese literature into other languages.

2.2.3 Perspectives of Translator's Style

The evolving translation theories and the emergence of a "cultural turn" in translation studies have significantly highlighted the importance of the translator's subjectivity. This shift has elevated the role of the translator from a "matchmaker" or "servant" to a central figure in the translation process. This literature review examines how the translator's style and subjectivity influence the translation of *The Scholars*.

The Emergence of Translator's Subjectivity

The translator's subjectivity has become increasingly prominent in translation studies. The realization that translators are not mere conduits for texts but play an integral role in shaping how a text is received and understood has revolutionized the field. This notion moves away from viewing the translator as a passive participant to acknowledging their active role in the cultural and literary interpretation.

The Influence of Translator's Style

Guo Mengyi (2015) conducts a comparative analysis of the two English versions of *The Scholars* translated by the Yangs and Zhang Xincang. Utilizing Steiner's fourfold translation motion, Guo discovers that the translators' writing style, cultural awareness, living environment, understanding of the original text, and translation purposes significantly influence their choice of translation strategies. This study illustrates that a translator's personal style and subjective interpretation play a crucial role in the translation process.

Explicitation and Implicitation

Zhu Sijuan (2012) explores the phenomena of explicitation and implicitation in the English translation of *The Scholars* from the perspective of the translator's subjectivity, rather than just linguistic factors. Zhu's research concludes that, apart from linguistic considerations, the translator's competence in source and target languages, ethical and moral values, aesthetic standards, cultural stance, and translation motivations greatly impact the use of explicitation or implicitation in translating linguistic and cultural elements.

Factors Influencing Translator's Subjectivity

Several factors contribute to the translator's subjectivity:

Cultural Awareness: A translator's cultural understanding profoundly influences how they interpret and translate a text. This includes knowledge of societal norms, historical context, and cultural nuances of both the source and target cultures.

Personal Aesthetics: Individual aesthetic preferences shape the stylistic choices a translator makes, affecting everything from word choice to sentence structure.

Ethical and Moral Values: A translator's ethical and moral standpoint can guide their decisions in translating sensitive or controversial content.

Translation Motivations: The purpose behind a translation, whether it be academic, commercial, or artistic, can steer a translator's approach and style.

The Role of Translator's Competence

A translator's competence in both the source and target languages is crucial. It determines their ability to understand the nuances of the original text and to convey its essence in the target language effectively. This competence is not limited to linguistic proficiency but also includes an understanding of cultural idioms, literary styles, and historical contexts.

The Impact of Living Environment

The living environment and personal experience of translators also shape their interpretative lens. Factors such as the socio-political climate, exposure to various cultures, and personal life experience can subtly influence how a translator perceives and translates a text.

Translation as a Reflective Practice

Translation is increasingly viewed as a reflective practice, where the translator engages with the text in a dynamic and interpretive manner. This approach recognizes that translation is not a straightforward process of linguistic substitution but a complex act of cultural and literary interpretation.

Challenges in Assessing Translator's Style

One of the challenges in studying translator's style is the subjective nature of this analysis. It can be difficult to quantify or systematically analyze how individual experience and perspectives influence translation choices. Furthermore, a translator's style might evolve over time, making it challenging to draw general conclusions about their approach.

Future Research Directions

Future research in this area could focus on developing methodologies for systematically analyzing the impact of a translator's subjectivity on translation. This could involve longitudinal studies tracking changes in a translator's style over time or comparative studies examining how different translators approach the same text.

The translator's style and subjectivity play a pivotal role in the translation of *The Scholars*. Factors like cultural awareness, personal aesthetics, ethical and moral values, and translation motivations all contribute to how a translator interprets and conveys the original text. Recognizing the influence of these factors is crucial for understanding the complexity of translation and for appreciating the unique contributions of individual translators to the field. As translation studies continue to evolve, the exploration of the translator's subjectivity will undoubtedly remain a vital area of research, offering rich insights into the art and science of translation.

2.2.4 Perspectives of Culture

The translation of *Ru Lin Wai Shi* into English has sparked significant scholarly interest, particularly regarding the cultural dimensions of this endeavor. This literature review collates and analyzes contributions that specifically address the cultural aspects of translating this quintessential Chinese literary work.

Cultural Nuances and Translation

The translation of *Ru Lin Wai Shi* has necessitated a deep engagement with the cultural nuances embedded in the text. Scholars have explored how cultural elements, from idioms to social customs, are handled in translation. This involves not just linguistic competence but also a profound understanding of the cultural context of the source material.

Hybridity and the Third Space in Cultural Translation

Yang Minzi (2012) applied Homi K. Bhabha's theory of cultural translation, focusing on the concepts of hybridity and the Third Space. This approach underscores the transformative potential of translation, where a new, hybrid cultural space is created. The English version of *Ru Lin Wai Shi* serves as a case study to illustrate how translators navigate between preserving the profundity of Chinese classics and making them accessible to a global audience.

Preserving Cultural Identity

Chen Li (2008) emphasized the importance of maintaining cultural identity in translation. The ecological, linguistic, social, religious, and material aspects of cultural translation are explored in the context of *The Scholars*. This perspective highlights the translator's role in promoting traditional Chinese culture while adapting to the expectations of a foreign audience.

Culture-Loaded Words and Their Translation

Wang Li (2004, 2005) investigated the challenges of translating culturally loaded words in *The Scholars*. These studies point out the difficulty of conveying the full spectrum of meaning and cultural significance inherent in certain terms and concepts from the source language to the target language.

Cultural Fidelity and Reader Reception

The translation of culturally specific elements involves a delicate balance between fidelity to the source culture and the target audience's comprehension. Studies have examined how translators deal with this tension, striving to create a version of the text that resonates with readers unfamiliar with the original cultural context while preserving its authenticity.

Sociocultural Context and Pragmatics

Duan Yan (2016) approached the translation from a sociological and pragmatic perspective, examining the identity concept of address forms in both the Chinese and English versions of *The Scholars*. This study sheds light on the subtle ways in which sociocultural nuances are reflected and sometimes altered in the translation process.

Intertextuality and Cultural Context

Zhang Yan Yu's (2013) application of intertextuality theory to *The Scholars* highlights the importance of understanding the interplay of various texts and cultural contexts in translation. The study shows how intertextual references carry specific cultural meanings that need to be effectively communicated in the translated work.

Cultural Representation and Ethical Considerations

The ethical responsibility of translators in representing a culture is a significant theme in the translation of *Ru Lin Wai Shi*. This involves questions of how faithfully a translator should adhere to the source text's cultural elements and the extent to which adaptation is permissible or necessary for the target audience's understanding.

The Role of Aesthetics in Cultural Translation

The aesthetic elements of a literary work, including its style and tone, are deeply rooted in culture. Studies have examined how the aesthetic qualities of *The Scholars* are conveyed in translation, addressing the challenge of transferring these cultural-aesthetic elements across linguistic and cultural boundaries.

The translation of *Ru Lin Wai Shi* into English is a rich field for examining the intricacies of cultural translation. The studies reviewed here demonstrate a keen awareness of the complexity involved in transferring not just the language but the cultural essence of this significant work. From exploring the strategies for handling culturally loaded words to understanding the role of hybridity and the Third Space in cultural translation, these scholarly contributions provide a nuanced understanding of the cultural dimensions in translating *Ru Lin Wai Shi*. They underscore the importance of respecting the source culture while making the work accessible and relatable to a global audience, thus bridging cultural divides and enhancing cross-cultural understanding.

2.2.5 Other Perspectives

In addition to the major perspectives previously discussed, several scholars have contributed unique insights into the translation studies of *The Scholars*, expanding the research angles and methodologies. This section synthesizes their contributions, highlighting the diversity and depth of scholarly engagement with the novel's translation.

Narrative and Sociological Analysis

Pan Huilan (2008) employed narrative theory to compare various chapters of *Ru Lin Wai Shi* and its English version. The study focused on whether the translation successfully transferred four essential aspects of narrative mood: focalization, speech presentation, narrative of events, and narrator. Pan concluded that the reconstruction of narrative mood in the translation preserved the original style and narrative characteristics, achieving equivalence in both content and form.

Duan Yan (2016) approached the translation from sociological and pragmatic identity theories. A qualitative and comparative analysis of the identity concept of address forms in the Chinese and English versions of *Ru Lin Wai Shi* was conducted. Duan's research found unconscious changes in the identity concept of address forms in the original text, highlighting the importance of considering a variety of source language factors in the translation of address forms.

Ecological and Functional Translation Approaches

Chen Li (2008) made a systematic analysis of ecological, linguistic, social, religious, and material aspects in the translation of Chinese literary works. Chen advocated for foreignization to maintain national cultural identity and promote traditional Chinese culture's global dissemination.

Similarly, Zhang Linhong (2016) used Relevance Theory as a framework to analyze the translation strategies of culturally loaded words in *The Scholars*. The study found that translators should seek optimal relevance by employing strategies like direct translation, substitution, and free translation to achieve the best translation effects.

Linguistic and Ethical Considerations

Tao Jiaqi and Gong Xiaobin (2016) studied the English translation of euphemisms in *The Scholars* from the perspective of Chesterman's translation ethics model. The study revealed the translation ethics behind euphemisms and provided insights for translating euphemisms into English.

Descriptive and Comparative Analysis

Tu Guoyuan and Yan Hongfu (2007) conducted a comparative analysis of the Chinese and English versions of *Ru Lin Wai Shi*, examining omissions and abstractions in the translations by Lin Yutang and Yang Xianyi. The study explored the reasons behind these phenomena and their impact on the faithfulness of the translation, cross-cultural communication, and reader reception.

Li Hui (2008), combining descriptive analysis with case studies, proved the application of Skopos theory in literary translation, offering a new theoretical perspective for evaluating and interpreting literary translations.

Cultural and Communicative Aspects

Li Xiao Hui (2007), using *The Scholars* as a case study, revealed translation strategies through a comparative analysis of culturally loaded words in Chinese and English, exploring the achievement of functional equivalence in cross-cultural communication.

Guo Xiaohui (2010) conducted a comparative analysis of the translation of official titles in the Chinese and English versions of *Ru Lin Wai Shi*. The study emphasized the significance of translating official titles and suggested a combination of communicative and semantic translation methods for accurately conveying cultural information.

Reader Reception and Aesthetics

Lin Sujie (2014) based her research on Reception Aesthetics, analyzing Yang Xianyi and Gladys Yang's English translation of *Ru Lin Wai Shi*. The study focused on the translation methods and strategies for culturally loaded words, aiming to align the reader's horizon of expectations with the source text and create an appropriate aesthetic distance to enhance reader interest.

He Xiaocui (2016), guided by Liu Miqing's modern translation aesthetics theory, discussed the formal and non-formal systems in the English translation of *Ru Lin Wai Shi*. The study found that the translators successfully maintained fidelity to the original while achieving linguistic beauty and artistic style in the translation.

Adaptation and Foreignization

Yu Haohan (2022) applied ecological translation theory to the translation of *Ru Lin Wai Shi*, focusing on three dimensions of adaptation to address challenges in classical book translation, enhancing the accuracy of core content transmission and overall communication effectiveness.

Song Yang (2022) explored the strategies of domestication and foreignization in literary translation, specifically analyzing Yang Xianyi's translation of *Ru Lin Wai Shi*. The study detailed the cultural loss in translation, including absolute and relative cultural deficits.

The diverse perspectives and methodologies in the translation studies of *Ru Lin Wai Shi* reflect the complexity and richness of this classical Chinese novel's translation into English. These studies not only contribute to the field of translation studies but also enhance the understanding of cross-cultural communication, showcasing the dynamic interplay between fidelity, adaptation, and the preservation of cultural nuances. The cumulative insights from these scholars provide a comprehensive view of the challenges and strategies involved in translating culturally rich texts like *The Scholars*, offering valuable guidance for future translation endeavors.

2.2.6 Summary

The scholarly examination of *The Scholars* has undergone a significant evolution, marked by breakthroughs in theoretical frameworks, research objects, and methodologies. This comprehensive survey reveals several key developments and persisting challenges in the field.

Expansion of Theoretical Frameworks

Initially, translation studies of *The Scholars* were predominantly technical. Researchers focused on direct methods and skills, analyzing literal and free translations, equivalence, and fidelity. However, recent studies have shifted towards a more theoretical approach. This transition reflects a broader cultural turn in translation studies, where theories such as hermeneutics and postcolonial translation theory have become integral to understanding the translation of *Ru Lin Wai Shi*. These theoretical lenses offer deeper insights into the cultural, political, and ideological underpinnings of translation processes and products.

Diverse Linguistic Levels and New Research Subjects

The scope of research has expanded to include multiple linguistic levels, such as appellations, rhetoric, and Chinese Xiehouyu (two-part allegorical sayings). This broadening of scope reflects a growing interest in the intricate linguistic features of *The Scholars*. Moreover, new research subjects have emerged, including the analysis of the translator's style, the text style, and the construction of interpersonal functions within the novel. These areas underscore the complexity of translation as an art form that extends beyond mere linguistic conversion to involve stylistic and functional considerations.

Shift in Research Perspective

The field has witnessed a significant change in research perspective. While traditional studies focused on equivalence, fidelity, and the binary of literal versus free translation, contemporary research has shifted attention to external factors influencing the translation process and the final product.

This includes exploring the socio-cultural and historical contexts in which the translation occurs, the target readers' expectations, and the broader cultural implications of translation choices. The intervention of translation corpus studies has enriched this perspective, enabling researchers to delve into the linguistic features of *The Scholars* and the external motivations affecting these features' forms.

Methodological Advancements

Methodological advancements, particularly the incorporation of translation corpora, have facilitated quantitative analysis, enhancing the scientific rigor and objectivity of studies on *The Scholars*. The repeatability and empirical nature of corpus-based studies allow for more systematic and comprehensive analyses of the text. This approach has opened avenues for exploring linguistic patterns, stylistic tendencies, and the nuances of meaning-making in translation.

Identified Weaknesses and Future Directions

Despite these advancements, several weaknesses in the field remain unaddressed. The current body of research is imbalanced, with a predominant focus on translation methods and skills but less on in-depth linguistic features and the translation style. For instance, areas such as translation norms still represent a gap in the literature. Moreover, most studies tend to concentrate on specific linguistic levels, often failing to provide a holistic analysis of the entire spectrum of linguistic features, translation style, and translation norms in *The Scholars*.

Addressing the Gaps

To address these gaps, future research needs to adopt a more balanced and in-depth approach. This includes expanding the focus beyond translation methods to encompass a comprehensive analysis of linguistic features, stylistic elements, and the broader norms guiding translation practices. Such an approach would not only contribute to a richer understanding of the translation of *The Scholars* but also provide valuable insights into the complexity of literary translation as a whole.

In summary, the study of the translation of *The Scholars* has made significant strides, moving from a predominantly technical focus to a more theoretically and methodologically sophisticated terrain. This evolution reflects the dynamic nature of translation studies as a field that continually adapts to new challenges and perspectives. The current research landscape, while marked by notable achievements, still presents opportunities for further exploration and depth, particularly in areas such as linguistic features, translation norms, and holistic analyses. Addressing these areas will not only fill existing gaps but also enrich our understanding of the interplay between language, culture, and translation in the context of this seminal Chinese literary work.

2.3 Previous Researches on Translation Norms

Translation norms represent a critical area of study in translation studies, encompassing a broad range of practices, theories, and methodologies. This review synthesizes key research themes and identifies gaps and potential directions in the study of translation norms.

Theoretical Foundations and Methodological Approaches

Toury (1995) and Hermans (2004) laid the groundwork for studying translation norms, providing theoretical frameworks that have guided much of the subsequent research. However, their theories, particularly Toury's, have faced criticism for their limited application to Hebrew translation and lack of empirical support.

Identification of Universal Features in Translated Languages

Researchers like Zhao Qiurong, Li Wenshuang (2024), Hu Kaibao(2011, 2015), and Tian Xujun (2023) have focused on identifying patterns and unique characteristics in translations. Their work moves from analyzing regularities in translated texts to examining the underlying motivations behind these patterns. This line of research attempts to discern universal features in translated languages, contributing significantly to our understanding of translation as a global practice.

Translation within Specialized Fields

Specialized fields pose unique challenges for translators, and researchers such as Hu Yuhuan (2024), Zhao Junfeng, Xue Jie, Zhang Wenlong (2023), and Liu Pu (2023) have explored these challenges. Their work examines the translation of specialized languages in fields like agriculture, legislation, and medical care, addressing the intricacies of terms, phrases, and expressions unique to these domains.

Pedagogical Translation Research

Studies by Li Chonghua, Zhang Zheng (2023), and Sun Xiaorong (2022) address translator training, focusing on the development of translation strategies and standards within educational contexts. This research pathway is crucial for shaping future generations of translators, ensuring they are well-equipped with the necessary skills and ethical standards.

Translation Technology and Ethics

The intersection of translation technology and ethics has become increasingly relevant. Researchers such as Wu Meixuan and Chen Hongjun (2023) explore the implications of artificial intelligence and machine translation on ethical dimensions. Their work challenges the traditional understanding of the translation process and its outcomes in the context of emerging technologies.

Socio-Cultural Impact of Translation

The socio-cultural impact of translation is a significant area of inquiry. Researchers like Hong Tao (2006), Liang Na, Li Yu, Zhang Xiaolin (2005), and Wang Qiusheng (2004) investigate how translations influence and reflect socio-cultural values and norms. This line of research contributes to the broader discourse on the role of translation in society, examining how translated texts can both shape and be shaped by the cultures they interact with.

Empirical Research and Cross-Disciplinary Integration

Current literature reveals fragmentation in empirical translation research and a need for cross-disciplinary integration. While individual studies provide valuable insights, there is a lack of consensus on theoretical frameworks and a limited focus on practical application. The field would benefit from more unified and systematic approaches that integrate descriptive and normative methodologies.

Potential New Research Directions

The current state of the field justifies several new research directions. A comprehensive framework for corpus-based translation studies could provide a more systematic and empirical approach to understanding translation norms. Additionally, integrated approaches that combine descriptive and normative methodologies could offer more holistic insights into translation practices. Finally, examining translation as a dynamic socio-cultural phenomenon would contribute to a more nuanced understanding of the role of translation in society.

In conclusion, the study of translation norms has evolved significantly, with researchers exploring a wide range of themes from theoretical foundations to practical applications. While the field has made considerable progress, it still faces challenges such as the need for more empirical research and cross-disciplinary integration. Future research directions offer promising pathways for addressing these challenges, contributing to the advancement of the field and the practice of translation globally.

Chapter Three

Theoretical Framework

This chapter lays out the theoretical framework underpinning the entire study, providing a comprehensive understanding of translation as a complex communicative action. Initially, it reinterprets the nature of translation behavior, viewing it not merely as a linguistic exchange but as a multifaceted communicative act that encompasses cultural, contextual, and interactive elements. This perspective broadens the traditional understanding of translation, emphasizing its role in facilitating cross-cultural dialogue and understanding.

Subsequently, the chapter delves into a redefinition of translation norms. These norms are not viewed as static rules but as dynamic guidelines that evolve with changing societal, cultural, and linguistic contexts. This redefinition recognizes the fluidity and adaptability of translation practices in response to varying communicative needs and environments.

Furthermore, the chapter proposes a reclassification of translation norms. It categorizes them into operational norms, which dictate the practical aspects of translation, and expectation norms, encompassing both convention expectation and foreignness expectation. This reclassification aims to provide a clearer understanding of the roles and responsibilities of translators, as well as the diverse standards they uphold in their practice to meet varying expectations in different cultural and linguistic contexts. This theoretical framework thus serves as a foundation for the subsequent analysis and discussions throughout the study, offering a fresh perspective on the complexity and nuances of translation as a communicative action.

3.1 Translation Behavior

Translation, a complex and nuanced process, transcends the simplistic view of merely converting text from one language into another. It embodies a dynamic interplay of linguistic precision, cultural sensitivity, and social awareness. The intricacy of this process is underscored by the rich theoretical framework provided by Jürgen Habermas's (2001) theory of communicative action. This theory, emanating from the intellectual rigor of one of Germany's most prominent social philosophers, offers an expansive lens through which the multifaceted nature of translation can be reevaluated and understood more deeply. Habermas's insights into mutual understanding and rational communication between individuals illuminate the core of what translation aims to achieve: not just a transfer of words, but a bridging of worlds.

At the heart of Habermas's communicative action theory lies the pursuit of mutual understanding and the facilitation of rational dialogue through the medium of language. This profound concept elevates communication beyond a mere exchange of information, inviting us to consider the underlying intentions, meanings, and cultural contexts that shape and are shaped by discourse. For the field of translation, this perspective is invaluable. It shifts the focus from a mechanical replication of text to a more holistic approach that respects and reflects the complexity of linguistic and cultural transference. This theoretical foundation emphasizes the translator's role as a mediator of meaning, tasked not only with navigating the nuances of language but also with bridging the gap between diverse cultural landscapes.

In applying Habermas's theory to translation studies, we are encouraged to view translation as a dialogic process that involves active engagement with both the source and target languages. This approach highlights the importance of understanding the socio-cultural contexts from which texts emerge and into which they are translated. It acknowledges that every act of translation is embedded within a web of social interactions and cultural meanings, necessitating a careful and considered approach to ensure that translations resonate with their new audiences without losing the essence of the original.

Furthermore, Habermas's emphasis on rational communication and the strive for mutual understanding brings to light the ethical dimensions of translation. It underscores the translator's responsibility not only to accurately convey the literal meaning of the source text but also to faithfully represent its intent and tone. This ethical imperative calls for a deep engagement with the text, requiring translators to interpret and then re-create the original message in a way that is both true to its essence and accessible to the target audience.

Moreover, the theory of communicative action enriches our understanding of translation by framing it as a collaborative endeavor. It positions the translator as a participant in a broader dialogue, one that extends beyond the text to include the original author, the target audience, and the cultural contexts that influence both the production and reception of translated works. This perspective fosters a sense of respect and empathy towards the source material, encouraging translators to approach their work with an awareness of the cultural and linguistic diversity that defines our globalized world.

In sum, Jürgen Habermas's communicative action theory offers a compelling theoretical backdrop against which the complexity of translation can be explored. By emphasizing mutual understanding, rational communication, and the ethical responsibilities of the translator, this theory provides a robust framework for examining the linguistic, cultural, and social dimensions of translation. It challenges us to view translation not as a mere linguistic exercise but as a vital act of cultural and communicative exchange, one that plays a crucial role in fostering understanding and connectivity in our increasingly interconnected world.

Translation norms serve as the bedrock upon which the act of translation is both grounded and guided, playing a critical role in ensuring that translations transcend mere linguistic fidelity to embody cultural and social appropriateness. These norms are inherently imbued with a social dimension, intricately weaving into the fabric of translation behavior and significantly influencing how translations are both executed by translators and received by the target culture. The concept of translation norms is multifaceted, shaped by a myriad of factors including, but not limited to, cultural conventions, societal expectations, and the ethical considerations that the translator brings into the translation process.

The Social Attribute of Translation Norms

Translation norms are not static; they are dynamic entities that evolve over time, influenced by the shifting sands of cultural conventions and societal expectations. They act as a bridge between the source and target cultures, facilitating a dialogue that is both meaningful and contextually relevant. The social attribute of these norms underscores the importance of understanding translation not just as a linguistic act but as a socio-cultural endeavor. This understanding necessitates a deep engagement with the norms that pervade the target culture, ensuring that the translation resonates with the audience not just linguistically but culturally and socially as well.

Communicative Action in Translation

Jürgen Habermas's theory of communicative action provides a robust framework for understanding the complex dynamics involved in the translation process. By applying this theory to translation, we delve into the nuanced relationship that the translator navigates between the world of the source text and the world of the target audience. This dual relationship underscores the multifaceted nature of translation, highlighting three critical dimensions:

The Objective World: This dimension involves the translator's engagement with the factual content and literal meaning of the source text. The objective world demands a meticulous approach to preserving the integrity of the source text's factual reality, requiring translators to tread the delicate balance between accuracy and adaptability.

The Social World: Translation is deeply embedded in the social fabric, necessitating an understanding of the cultural and societal norms that govern acceptable behavior and communication within both the source and target cultures. The social world dimension emphasizes the translator's role in mediating between cultures, necessitating a sensitivity to the norms, values, and expectations that define the target culture.

The Subjective World: At the heart of the translation process lies the subjective world of the translator. This dimension acknowledges the personal interpretations, biases, and creative choices that the translator brings to the translation. It highlights the subjective nature of translation, where the translator's personal experience, cultural background, and ethical considerations shape the translation outcome.

Principles of Communicative Rationality in Translation

Habermas's principles of communicative rationality offer valuable insights into the ethical and practical considerations inherent in the translation process. These principles underscore the multifaceted responsibilities of translators, guiding their approach to achieving a translation that is not only linguistically accurate but also culturally and socially resonant.

Intelligibility: The principle of intelligibility stresses the importance of creating a translation that is accessible and understandable to the target audience. This requires a nuanced approach, balancing the need for literal accuracy with the imperative for cultural adaptation. Intelligibility is crucial for ensuring that the translation communicates the intended message in a way that is clear and comprehensible.

Truth: The commitment to truth demands that translators convey the factual reality of the source text with integrity and authenticity. This principle challenges translators to navigate the complexity of the source text, ensuring that the translation accurately reflects its factual content without distortion.

Sincerity: Sincerity in translation involves a genuine representation of the source text's emotions, intentions, and meanings. This principle emphasizes the ethical responsibility of translators to faithfully interpret and convey the essence of the source text, respecting its original context and intent.

Normative Rightness: Adherence to the principle of normative rightness requires translations to align with the ethical, cultural, and societal norms of the target culture. This principle underscores the need for cultural sensitivity, ensuring that translations are not only linguistically accurate but also respectful of the target culture's values and expectations.

The application of Habermas's principles of communicative rationality to translation illuminates the ethical landscape that translators navigate. It highlights the imperative for translations to achieve a balance between linguistic fidelity, cultural sensitivity, and ethical responsibility. These principles serve as a guiding light, ensuring that translations fulfill their role as bridges between cultures, facilitating understanding, and fostering cross-cultural dialogue.

Translators stand at the crossroads of languages and cultures, serving not merely as conduits for text conversion but as vital participants in a nuanced communication process. Their task involves a sophisticated dance between the objective reality of the source text, the woven tapestry of social expectations across both source and target cultures, and their own subjective interpretations. This intricate navigation demands more than linguistic acumen; it requires a deep empathy for and understanding of the cultural and emotional landscapes encoded in the language.

Navigating the Objective Reality

The translator's first allegiance is to the truth of the source text. This demands a meticulous approach to understanding its factual content, historical context, and the author's intentions. However, fidelity to the source is not a straightforward task of literal translation but a complex decision-making process. Translators must decipher the nuances of the original language and choose equivalent expressions in the target language that convey the same meaning, tone, and impact.

Bridging Social Expectations

The cultural and societal norms governing communication within both the source and target cultures significantly influence translation. Translators act as cultural mediators, interpreting and adapting the source text to align with the target audience's expectations and norms. This role requires a deep cultural intelligence and the ability to anticipate how translations will be received and understood by different audiences. Translators must navigate the fine line between preserving the cultural essence of the source text and making it accessible and relevant to the target culture.

Embracing Subjectivity

While striving for objectivity and fidelity to the source, translators inevitably bring their subjective interpretations to the translation process. Their personal experience, biases, and creative choices color the translation, making each one a unique interpretation of the original. This subjectivity is not a flaw but a feature of the translation process, adding depth and richness to the translated text. It underscores the translator's role not just as a linguistic expert but as an interpreter of meaning.

Socio-Cultural Contexts and Constraints

Translation does not occur in a vacuum but is deeply embedded in specific socio-cultural contexts. Translators navigate a landscape riddled with linguistic challenges, cultural differences, and societal expectations. This environment necessitates not only a linguistic translation but a cultural one, requiring translators to possess a profound understanding of the cultures at play.

Linguistic Challenges

The linguistic nuances of the source text, including idioms, metaphors, and culturally specific references, present significant challenges. Translators must find ways to convey these elements in the target language, often requiring creative solutions to preserve the original's meaning and tone.

Cultural Differences

Cultural differences encompass more than just language; they include values, beliefs, and practices that can significantly impact translation. Translators must be sensitive to these differences, adapting the source text in ways that respect the target culture while staying true to the original's essence.

Societal Expectations

Societal expectations and norms influence what is considered acceptable or offensive in both the source and target cultures. Translators must be aware of these norms to ensure that their translations are appropriate and respectful, navigating the potential for misunderstanding or controversy.

Ethical Considerations in Translation

The ethical dimension of translation is intertwined with the principle of normative rightness, challenging translators to make ethical decisions about representing sensitive content, handling cultural differences, and maintaining the source text's integrity.

Representing Sensitive Content

Translators frequently encounter sensitive or controversial material that requires careful handling. Decisions on how to translate such content involve balancing fidelity to the original with sensitivity to the target audience's potential reactions.

Handling Cultural Differences

Ethical translation involves more than linguistic accuracy; it requires cultural sensitivity and respect. Translators must navigate cultural differences with care, avoiding stereotyping, misrepresentation, and cultural appropriation.

Maintaining Integrity

Maintaining the integrity of the source text while making it accessible to a new audience is a core ethical challenge. Translators must decide how to adapt the text without distorting its original meaning, a task that requires both ethical judgment and creative skill.

The Creative Aspect of Translation

Translation is inherently a creative act. Translators bring their linguistic skills, cultural knowledge, and personal experience to bear on the process, interpreting the source text and recreating it in a new cultural and linguistic context. This creative aspect highlights the translation's subjective nature, emphasizing the unique contribution of each translator.

Conclusion

Viewing translation through the lens of communicative action, as proposed by Jürgen Habermas, enriches our understanding of the translation process. It illuminates the complex interplay between linguistic fidelity, cultural sensitivity, and ethical considerations, underscoring the translator's pivotal role in facilitating cross-cultural communication. This perspective reveals translation as a deeply social and subjective behavior, influenced by a multitude of factors beyond mere words. Translators emerge not just as linguistic experts but as cultural mediators and creative interpreters, tasked with bridging worlds and fostering understanding across the tapestry of human culture.

3.2 Translation Norms

Definition of Translation Norms

The concept of norms within the realm of translation studies is both complex and multifaceted, drawing from deep sociological roots that intertwine with the notions of morality, ethics, and legality. As articulated by Fu Jingmin (2013), the exploration into norms transcends a mere academic exercise, positioning itself at the confluence of societal expectations and the ethical imperatives that govern behavior. This foundational understanding sets the stage for a nuanced discussion within translation studies, significantly influenced by scholars like Gideon Toury, Andrew Chesterman, and Theo Hermans, each of whom has contributed to the evolution of norm theory from distinct yet complementary perspectives.

Gideon Toury's Perspective on Translation Norms

Gideon Toury's pioneering work in the early 1980s laid the groundwork for the conceptualization of norms in translation studies. Toury perceived norms as a category vital for the descriptive analysis of translation phenomena, a perspective that underscores the importance of understanding translation activities within their social and cultural milieu. According to Toury, norms represent the translation of general values or ideas prevalent within a community into specific performance instructions tailored to particular contexts. This approach highlights the translator's role in navigating between the expectations of the source and target cultures, making practical choices that align with the shared values of the target community. Toury's emphasis on practicality in translation choices reflects an understanding of translation as an act deeply embedded in social context, where decisions are influenced by a broader cultural consensus on what constitutes right and wrong, adequate and inadequate.

Theo Hermans's Focus on Behavioral Regularity

Theo Hermans expanded the discussion on norms by focusing on the dual nature of the term: as a descriptor of regularities in behavior and as a mechanism accounting for such regularities. Hermans's interpretation broadens the scope of norms to include the underlying systems that engender consistent patterns in translation behavior. This perspective shifts the focus from the micro-level specifics of translation choices to a macro-level analysis of how norms influence translation as a whole. Hermans's approach does not prioritize textual fidelity between the original and translated works; instead, it emphasizes the disparities in rights and values that different texts embody, bringing to light the manipulative essence of translation.

Andrew Chesterman's Notion of Norms as Social Reality

Andrew Chesterman's contribution further enriches the discourse on norms by framing them as manifestations of the social reality of correctness notions within specific communities. Chesterman argues that norms should not be understood as directives issued from a hierarchical structure but as descriptions of practices that prevail within a given community. This perspective underscores the influence of the target language and culture on the translator's choices, highlighting the social dimensions of translation activity. Chesterman's emphasis on the social reality of norms points to the communal and negotiated nature of translation practices, where norms serve as a guiding framework rather than prescriptive rules.

Hu Xianyao's Definition of Translation Norms

Synthesizing these diverse perspectives, Hu Xianyao offers a definition of translation norms that encapsulates their essence as the social reality of the correctness of translation. According to Hu, norms represent the collective knowledge within a sociocultural context about the proper conduct of translation. This definition acknowledges that norms are acquired through the process of socialization, bearing the weight of societal pressures and sanctions, and manifesting through regularities in translational activities. Hu's definition emphasizes the communal aspect of norms, highlighting how they are internalized by translators and reflected in their work.

Conclusion

The exploration of norms within translation studies reveals a rich tapestry of theoretical insights that illuminate the complex interplay between translation as a practice and the societal frameworks that shape it. From Toury's emphasis on practical choices to Hermans's focus on behavioral regularities, and Chesterman's exploration of social realities, the discourse on norms encompasses a broad spectrum of considerations that influence translation. Hu Xianyao's synthesis of these perspectives provides a comprehensive definition that encapsulates the multifaceted nature of norms as both a product and a reflection of the sociocultural context in which translation occurs. As the field of translation studies continues to evolve, the concept of norms remains a pivotal area of inquiry, offering profound implications for understanding translation as a socially embedded practice that navigates between the demands of fidelity, ethics, and cultural sensitivity.

The discourse on translation norms has seen significant contributions from scholars like Toury (1995), Chesterman (2012), and Nord (1991), each offering unique perspectives and classifications that enrich our understanding of translation practices. However, a critical analysis suggests that while these classifications are insightful, there appears to be a disconnect between the proposed categories of norms and the methodologies employed in their research. This gap highlights the complexity of applying theoretical classifications to practical translation studies and underscores the need for a more integrated approach.

Enter Hu Xianyao (2006), who revolutionizes this field by marrying the study of translation norms with corpus linguistics, presenting a novel breakthrough in research methodology. In his seminal work, *A Corpus-Based Study on the Translational Norms of Contemporary Chinese Translated Fiction*, Hu proposes a bifurcation of translation norms into two distinct categories. This approach not only provides a clear framework for analyzing translation practices but also leverages the empirical strength of corpus analysis to ground theoretical insights in observable data. Hu's methodology signifies a pivotal advancement in translation studies, bridging the gap between norm classification and research methodology, and setting a new standard for future inquiries into the nature and impact of translation norms. The detailed classification is as follows:

Table 3.1　The Classification of Translation Norms (Hu Xianyao,2006:95)

External Norms	selection norms	the selection of text, source language and translator/ interpreter
	expectation norms	convention expectation
		foreignness expectation
Internal Norms	accountability norms	translators owe loyalty to the readers,original writers,and agent of the translation job
	communication norms	translators coordinate effective communication among writers, readers and agents
	operation norms	lexical operation norms
		syntactic operation norms

In exploring the multifaceted nature of translation norms, it becomes evident that these norms can be broadly categorized into external and internal ones, based on the entities that establish them. External norms, as shaped by readers and societal institutions, delineate the broader expectations placed upon translations. They encompass selection norms, which dictate the choice of texts, source languages, and translators or interpreters, highlighting the strategic considerations behind translation endeavors. Additionally, expectation norms, a subset of external norms, address the translational conceptualizations held by specific cultural groups. These are further divided into convention expectation, where there is an anticipation for the translated texts to adhere to the linguistic and cultural traditions of the target audience, thereby being "target-language oriented" or "domestication-oriented". In contrast, foreignness expectation pivots towards a curiosity and desire to engage with the unfamiliar, encouraging translations that retain the essence of the source language and culture, thus being "source-language oriented" or "foreignism-oriented".

Conversely, internal norms are established by professional translators themselves, encompassing accountability norms that stress the translator's fidelity to the source author, the readers, and the translation job's agents. Communication norms emphasize the translator's role in facilitating effective interaction among the author, the readers, and other stakeholders, ensuring that the translation serves its intended communicative purpose. Operation norms focus on achieving a suitable relationship of relevance and similarity between the source and target texts, with specific considerations for lexical and syntactic choices that directly influence the translation's linguistic features.

This study aims to delve into the expectation and operation norms, employing corpus tools and methodologies to dissect the characteristics of *The Scholars*. Through this analytical lens, the study will explore how these norms manifest in the English version of *Ru Lin Wai Shi*, seeking to understand the balance between foreignness and convention expectations and how it shapes the translated work.

Chapter Four

Research Methodology

This chapter delineates the methodological framework and research design meticulously crafted to interrogate the research questions posited at the outset. To unravel these inquiries, a corpus-based methodology is advocated, offering a robust pathway to derive insightful answers. This approach underpins the research design, which commences with a detailed explication of the principal methods employed. These include analyses focusing on the degrees of explicitness versus implicitness, simplification versus complication, normalization versus deviation, as well as parataxis versus hypotaxis, and lastly, the investigation of sanitization versus contamination within translations. Following this, the chapter unfolds to reveal a comprehensive illustration of the data collection and analysis phases. This section meticulously outlines the procedural steps undertaken, from the initial gathering of corpus data to the systematic examination and interpretation of findings, thereby ensuring a thorough and nuanced understanding of the translational phenomena under study.

4.1 Research Questions

1)Which translation norms can be identified within *The Scholars*?

2)Why were these specific norms chosen for use in the translation?

4.2 Research Approach: Corpus-Driven Approach

As highlighted in the preceding chapter, research endeavors focusing on translation norms have traditionally leaned towards qualitative methodologies, offering rich, in-depth insights into the subjective interpretations and contextual applications of these norms. Despite the invaluable perspectives garnered through qualitative research, the introduction of quantitative methodologies promises to enhance the objectivity and scientific rigor of such studies. Quantitative approaches, characterized by their repeatability, enable a broader and more empirical examination of data, thereby lending a complementary dimension to the inherently interpretive nature of qualitative analysis. Consequently, marrying qualitative insights with quantitative data analysis not only enriches the comprehensiveness of the research outcomes but also ensures a more balanced and robust investigation. This synergistic integration of methodologies finds its most effective expression through the use of corpus-based studies, which adeptly bridge the qualitative and quantitative realms, offering a holistic view of translation norms in practice.

In the development of this research paper, the author has strategically selected AntConc[1] and PowerGREP[2] as the primary tools for data analysis, leveraging their advanced capabilities to conduct an in-depth corpus linguistics and corpus-based translation studies. AntConc, a sophisticated online freeware meticulously crafted by Dr. Laurence Anthony, a distinguished professor with a specialization in educational technology, stands out for its user-friendly interface and comprehensive suite of functionalities. It equips researchers with a robust set of features including concordance, concordance plot, file view, clusters, collocates, word list, and keyword list, making it an indispensable tool in the arsenal of many scholars engaged in linguistic research.

On the other hand, PowerGREP emerges as a formidable grep tool for Windows, renowned for its ability to swiftly sift through vast arrays of files, whether they are stored locally on a PC or across a network. This tool's versatility extends to a wide variety of file types, encompassing text and binary files, compressed archives, MS Word documents, Excel spreadsheets, PDF files, and Open Office files, among others. PowerGREP's prowess is not limited to mere search functionality; it excels in applying regular expressions for advanced searches and data extraction from files. In the context of this thesis, PowerGREP has been instrumental in presenting key sentences from *The Scholars* in a parallel format, thereby facilitating a comprehensive contrastive linguistic analysis. This dual-tool approach, combining the intuitive analysis capabilities of AntConc with the extensive search and extraction functionalities of PowerGREP, ensures a methodologically sound and nuanced exploration of translation norms within *The Scholars*.

To rigorously analyze the translation norms in *The Scholars*, a meticulously structured parallel corpus is being constructed, with the foundational texts meticulously selected from the esteemed *Library of Chinese Classics* (1999). This collection serves as a critical resource, providing a reliable foundation for sourcing both the original Chinese text and its English counterpart. To ensure a robust and representative sample, random sampling methodology will be employed to select 42 chapters[3] from *The Scholars*, thereby capturing the diverse linguistic and cultural nuances inherent in this seminal work.

To facilitate the intricate process of aligning the source and target texts at a granular sentence level, Tmxmall[4], an advanced online alignment tool, will be utilized. This tool specializes in generating alignments in .txt format, allowing for precise and efficient analysis. Alongside the parallel corpus, a comparable corpus is also in development, aiming to meticulously match the original and translated texts in several key aspects. These aspects include register, size, and publication time, ensuring a high degree of similarity and relevance for comparative analysis, as emphasized by Hu Kaibao (2011).

Catch-22 has been strategically chosen as the reference corpus for this comparative study, owing to its thematic and stylistic resemblances to *The Scholars*. This choice is grounded in the need to analyze texts that share similarities in linguistic register, length, and temporal context, thereby providing a coherent framework for examining translational norms. The foundational data for both corpora will be meticulously compiled, setting the stage for an in-depth exploration of translation practices and norms as they manifest in these culturally and linguistically rich texts. The basic data of the two corpora are as follows:

Table 4.1 English Comparable Corpus

	Catch-22	***The Scholars***
Register	literature	literature
Tokens	179,959	181,951
Publication Time	1961	1957

The comparative analysis of *Catch-22* and *The Scholars* reveals a striking similarity in their dimensions, making them highly comparable for the purposes of this study. *Catch-22*, with its word count of 179,959 and publication year of 1961, closely mirrors *The Scholars*, which boasts a slightly larger word count of 181,951 and was published slightly earlier, in 1957. Both texts, rooted firmly in the literary genre, exhibit minimal disparities, thus providing a solid foundation for comparative analysis. This close alignment in size and temporal context, coupled with their literary nature, ensures their suitability for a side-by-side evaluation. The parallel corpus serves a critical function in juxtaposing the translation directly with the original text, enabling a nuanced examination of translational choices and fidelity. Conversely, the comparable corpus facilitates an investigation into how the translated version of *The Scholars* stands in relation to *Catch-22*, a non-translated work of similar literary value and time period, thereby shedding light on the distinctive features in translation versus non-translation literature.

4.3 Research Design

When applying corpus methodology to research, it entails a structured approach that includes three foundational layers: selecting the data source, meticulously collecting the data, and rigorously analyzing the data to extract meaningful insights.

4.3.1 Data Sources

In his seminal work, *A Corpus-Based Study on the Translational Norms of Contemporary Chinese Translated Fiction*, Hu Xianyao (2006) set forth a groundbreaking methodology for investigating translation norms through corpus analysis. This approach has inspired the current research, which aims to delve into the operational norms within translation, examining key assumptions such as explicitness versus implicitness, simplification versus complication, parataxis versus hypotaxis, normalization versus deviation, and sanitization versus contamination. This investigation will scrutinize the lexical and syntactic characteristics of translated texts, including lexical variability, the distinctive features of parts of speech, various translation methods, and the specific uses of conjunctions. Through this detailed analysis, the study seeks to distill the underlying expectation norms, offering a nuanced understanding of the standards and conventions that guide translation practices. By adapting Hu's corpus methodology, this research endeavors to shed light on the complex interplay between operational norms and their manifestation in the lexical and syntactic choices of translators, thereby contributing to a deeper comprehension of translation norms in contemporary Chinese translated fiction.

Exploring the intricate dynamics of translation norms, particularly through the lenses of parataxis versus hypotaxis and explicitness versus implicitness, reveals profound insights into the complex interplay between source and target languages, in this case, Chinese and English. These linguistic structures and translational choices not only reflect the grammatical and syntactic differences between languages but also embody the cultural and stylistic expectations that shape translation practices.

Parataxis or Hypotaxis

Parataxis and hypotaxis represent fundamental structural divergences between Chinese and English, influencing how ideas and clauses are connected within texts. Parataxis, characterized by the sequential arrangement of clauses without explicit markers of their relationship, is a prevalent feature in Chinese, reflecting a stylistic preference for a more direct, linear narrative flow. In contrast, English often employs hypotaxis, which integrates clauses and expressions through linguistic forms such as affixes, inflectional words, connectives, and prepositions, thereby elucidating grammatical and logical relationships more explicitly.

The translator's approach to navigating these divergent structures is significantly influenced by prevailing translation norms, which oscillate between favoring convention and foreignness. When translation norms lean towards tradition and formality, translations exhibit a higher degree of hypotaxis, marked by an increased use of conjunctions, relative words, and more complex syntactic structures. This adherence to formality aligns with convention expectation, aiming to render the text more palatable to the target language's readers by conforming to its grammatical and stylistic norms. Conversely, a predilection for parataxis signifies a departure from this formality, resulting in translations characterized by fewer conjunctions, simpler syntactic constructions, and a stylistic looseness that mirrors the source language's structure. This approach, influenced by foreignness expectation, seeks to preserve the source text's uniqueness, potentially at the expense of readability in the target language.

Explicitness or Implicitness

The concepts of explicitness and implicitness delve deeper into the translator's role in clarifying or maintaining the implicit information embedded in the source text. "Explicitation" refers to the process of rendering implicit or vague information in the source text into clear, unambiguous expressions in the translation, enhancing the reader's comprehension. This translational characteristic aligns with convention expectation, where the goal is to adapt the text to fit the linguistic and cultural norms of the target audience, thereby facilitating acceptance and understanding.

In contrast, "implicitness" maintains the source text's subtlety, preserving its original nuances and the "foreignness" that might intrigue or challenge the target audience. This approach reflects foreignness expectation, where the translation retains the source language's idiosyncrasies, potentially compromising clarity for the sake of authenticity. The preference for explicitness or implicitness in a given period is indicative of the underlying expectation norms, with more traditional norms favoring explicitation to ensure clarity and coherence, and foreign-oriented norms embracing implicitness to maintain the source text's cultural and linguistic integrity.

The translation of texts from one period to another can thus be seen as a reflection of the prevailing norms of that era. Translations governed by traditional norms tend to be more explicit, with longer sentences and paragraphs that aim to convey the source text's meaning as transparently as possible. Conversely, translations influenced by a preference for foreignness are likely to be less explicit, characterized by brevity in sentence and paragraph length, which may challenge the reader's understanding but also enrich their experience by exposing them to the linguistic and cultural depth of the source text.

In summary, the exploration of parataxis versus hypotaxis and explicitness versus implicitness within translation norms provides a nuanced understanding of how translators navigate the complex terrain between fidelity to the source text and adaptability to the target audience's expectations. These translational choices are emblematic of broader cultural, linguistic, and stylistic considerations that define the art and science of translation, highlighting the translator's pivotal role in bridging disparate languages and cultures.

In the nuanced domain of translation studies, the concepts of simplification versus complication, and normalization versus deviation, stand as pivotal considerations that reveal much about the underlying norms and expectations guiding translators' choices. These dimensions are not merely stylistic preferences but are deeply entwined with the cultural, historical, and linguistic contexts of both source and target texts, reflecting broader societal expectations and norms within specific periods.

Simplification or Complication

Simplification in translation is often seen as a subconscious effort by translators to make the source text more accessible to the target culture's audience. According to Hu Kaibao (2011), this process might involve reducing the lexical density of the text, opting for more common words over less frequent ones, and favoring functional words while minimizing content-heavy words. The essence of simplification lies in two main aspects: lexical and syntactic. Lexically, simplification might manifest through the preference for hypernyms over hyponyms, signaling a shift towards generality rather than specificity. Syntactically, it involves streamlining complex sentence structures, breaking down lengthy sentences, and removing redundant elements to enhance readability and comprehension.

Conversely, complication as a translation strategy adheres closely to the original text's wording, syntactic structure, and lexical choices, even at the cost of increased difficulty for the target audience. This approach retains the source text's complexity, including its use of unique, extraordinary, or archaic terms and its intricate phrases and sentence patterns. Complication, therefore, is not merely about preserving the linguistic features of the original but also about maintaining its historical depth, semantic richness, and the "foreignness" that might be inherent in its form.

The choice between simplification and complication reflects the translator's navigation between convention and foreignness expectations. Simplification aims to enhance the translated text's acceptability, aligning it more closely with the target language's conventions and cultural norms. However, this approach may also result in the dilution of the original text's historical context, semantic depth, and distinctive form. In contrast, complication preserves these elements, aligning the translation with foreignness expectations but potentially making it less accessible to the target audience.

Normalization or Deviation

Normalization in translation is the process of aligning the translated text with the target language's conventions, including its punctuation, wording, stylistics, sentence structure, and textual organization. This approach seeks to produce translations that are readable, accurate, and grammatically aligned with the target language, often at the expense of the source text's unique cultural words, creative expressions, and non-standard syntactic constructions. Normalization, akin to domestication, emphasizes adaptability to the target culture's linguistic norms, "Do as the Romans do," making the translated text appear as though it were originally written in the target language.

Deviation, on the other hand, emphasizes the preservation of the source text's uniqueness, deliberately employing special words, loanwords, and maintaining the original's errors and illogicalities. This strategy, similar to foreignization, results in translations that may challenge or even violate the grammatical norms of the target language, retaining the original's peculiar language structure and cultural specificity.

The dynamic interplay between normalization and deviation in translation reflects the ongoing tension between the desire to conform to target language norms and the impulse to preserve the source text's distinctiveness. If the prevailing translation norms of a specific period lean towards normalization, translations from that period will likely conform more closely to the target language's rules, minimizing the original's uniqueness. Conversely, a period characterized by a preference for deviation will produce translations that foreground the source text's distinct qualities, even at the risk of reduced readability and acceptability.

In conclusion, the exploration of simplification versus complication, and normalization versus deviation, within translation practices offers profound insights into the complex decisions translators make to balance fidelity to the source text with the cultural and linguistic expectations of the target audience. These strategies reveal the deep-seated norms that shape translation choices, reflecting broader cultural, historical, and linguistic contexts that influence how translations are received and understood.

Sanitization and contamination within the realm of translation studies address the nuanced and often contentious decisions translators make regarding the inclusion or exclusion of material that could potentially conflict with the target culture's norms, values, and sensibilities. These terms encapsulate the translator's handling of expressions that might be deemed offensive or inappropriate within the target language context, including but not limited to slang, explicit sexual descriptions, ideologies that counter those predominant in the target culture, and depictions of religious beliefs that might clash with mainstream doctrines.

The process of sanitization involves a deliberate cleansing of the source text, where elements considered taboo[5] or controversial—such as references to sexual orientation, sexual practices outside societal norms, incest, or narratives that challenge the target culture's dominant ideologies—are meticulously removed or altered. This practice stems from a perceived need to protect the cultural purity and moral integrity of the target audience, ensuring that the translated work adheres to the prevailing ethical, cultural, and religious standards.

Conversely, contamination embraces the raw and unfiltered essence of the source text, retaining its original expressions, cultural references, and ideological stances, even when they diverge sharply from the target culture's conventions. This approach reflects a commitment to preserving the authenticity and integrity of the source material, allowing the target audience to engage with the text in its unadulterated form, thereby fostering a deeper understanding of the source culture's complexity and nuances.

The decision to sanitize or contaminate a translation is heavily influenced by the prevailing translation norms of a given period, which themselves are shaped by broader cultural, historical, and ideological currents. In eras characterized by more traditionalist translation norms, there is a marked preference for sanitization, resulting in translations that are carefully purged of content deemed objectionable or provocative. This tendency towards sanitization aligns with convention expectation, prioritizing the cultural and moral sensibilities of the target audience over the source text's original content and intent.

In contrast, periods marked by a more open and experimental approach to translation may exhibit a greater inclination towards contamination, allowing the translations to retain their original elements, even those that challenge or contravene the target culture's norms. This approach aligns with foreignness expectation, valuing the preservation of the source culture's identity and offering the target audience an unvarnished insight into its ideological, ethical, and cultural landscape.

The interplay between sanitization and contamination, and their relationship to translation norms, reveals a complex and dynamic tension between the desire to adapt texts to fit the cultural and moral frameworks of the target audience and the imperative to maintain the source text's integrity and authenticity. This tension underscores the translator's role as both a mediator between cultures and a gatekeeper of cultural and ideological exchange.

In summary, the approach adopted in this research posits that translations manifesting characteristics such as explicitness, simplification, parataxis, normalization, and sanitization tend towards convention expectation, reflecting a preference for adapting the source text to conform to the target culture's norms and values. Conversely, translations that exhibit features like implicitness, complication, hypotaxis, deviation, and contamination lean towards foreignness expectation, emphasizing the preservation of the source text's original qualities and allowing for a more direct encounter with its cultural and ideological complexity. This nuanced understanding of operation norms and their implications for translation practices provides a framework for analyzing how translations navigate the delicate balance between adaptation and authenticity. The research process is shown in Figure 4.1.

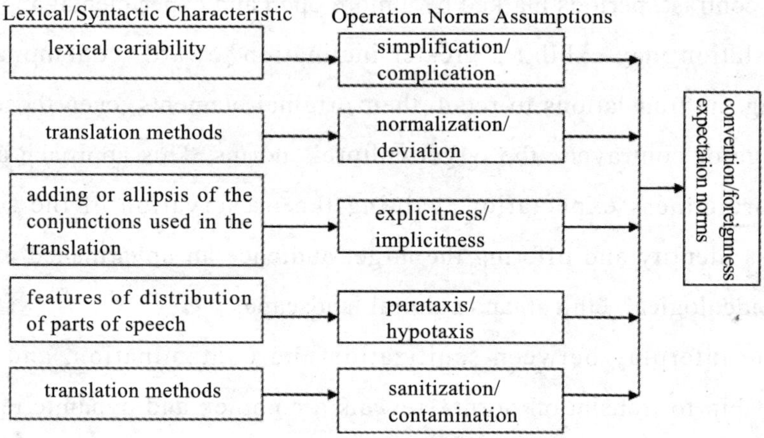

Figure 4.1 Research Process of the Translation Norms

Figure 4.1 delineates a comprehensive framework for the data collection strategy in this study, identifying five pivotal sources: explicitness versus implicitness, simplification versus complication, normalization versus deviation, parataxis versus hypotaxis, and sanitization versus contamination. These criteria are instrumental in dissecting and understanding the underlying expectation norms within *The Scholars*. This approach is methodically designed to excavate and analyze the nuanced translation practices, offering a multifaceted lens through which the expectation norms guiding the translation of *The Scholars* can be meticulously explored and understood.

4.3.2 Data Collection and Analysis

The methodology for data collection and analysis within this study is intricately designed to align with the specific research questions posited and the methods adopted by the researcher for data gathering. A crucial part of this approach involves an in-depth examination of the operational norms which are central to understanding the translational choices made in *The Scholars*.

4.3.2.1 The Data Collection and Analysis of Operation Norms

In this segment of the research, the focus will be on rigorously analyzing the operational norms underpinning the translation process. This analysis will be grounded in the exploration of five key assumptions: explicitness versus implicitness, simplification versus complication, convention versus foreignness, parataxis versus hypotaxis, and sanitization versus contamination. Each of these dimensions will be meticulously examined to uncover how they manifest in the translation of *Ru Lin Wai Shi*, thereby offering insights into the translational strategies employed. This process aims not only to identify the prevailing operational norms but also to understand how these norms influence the translation's fidelity to the source text, its accessibility to the target audience, and its adherence to or deviation from the cultural and linguistic expectations of the target language community.

This research endeavors to meticulously analyze the translation practices in *The Scholars* through a comprehensive corpus-based study, focusing on key operational norms such as explicitness/implicitness, simplification/complication, normalization/deviation, parataxis/hypotaxis, and sanitization/contamination. Each of these areas is crucial for understanding the nuanced translation strategies employed, and the methods for data collection and analysis are tailored to reveal the intricacies of these practices.

a. The Data Collection and Analysis of Explicitness/Implicitness

The explicitness/implicitness dimension investigates how translators navigate the balance between conveying implied information and omitting explicitly stated messages. Utilizing a Chinese-English parallel corpus of *The Scholars*, this analysis begins by examining the translation of Chinese connectives into English, providing a statistical basis for understanding the degree of implicitness. This approach not only highlights the translational choices made but also sheds light on the cultural and contextual factors influencing these decisions.

b. The Data Collection and Analysis of Simplification/Complication

To explore the tendency towards simplification or complication in translation, this study employs a comparative analysis of the source and translated texts, focusing on their type-token ratio (TTR). The TTR offers insights into lexical diversity, with a higher TTR indicating a greater variety of words used. This metric, however, is adjusted to account for corpus size, adopting a standardized type/token ratio. By examining the simplification of language through the lens of TTR, we can gauge the translator's approach to making the text more accessible or retaining its complexity.

c. The Data Collection and Analysis of Normalization/Deviation

Normalization and deviation are analyzed through the translation of idioms, a key element that reflects adherence to or departure from the target or source language culture. Idioms are categorized into two-part allegorical sayings, colloquialisms, proverbs, and set phrases. Using PowerGREP 4 for extraction, this research meticulously classifies and analyzes the translation of these idioms to determine the prevalence of normalization or deviation.

This step-by-step approach allows for a detailed understanding of how idiomatic expressions are handled in translation, revealing the translator's cultural alignment.

d. The Data Collection and Analysis of Parataxis/Hypotaxis

The study of parataxis versus hypotaxis focuses on the linguistic structures that indicate whether *The Scholars* relies on internal meaning or logical relationships for implicit connections, or on external linguistic forms for explicit connections. By examining the distribution features of parts of speech, this analysis aims to uncover the underlying grammatical and syntactic preferences in the translation, providing insights into the structural choices that shape the translated text.

e. The Data Collection and Analysis of Sanitization or Contamination

Sanitization versus contamination examines how translations handle potentially sensitive or culturally specific content, specifically religious terms in *The Scholars*. Selecting key religious words as search terms, this research calculates the frequency of different English translation methods used. This analysis seeks to understand how translators navigate the operation norms of sanitization or contamination, reflecting broader cultural and ethical considerations in the translation process.

This comprehensive methodological approach, encompassing five critical aspects of translation norms, aims to provide a nuanced understanding of the strategies and decisions underlying the translation of *Ru Lin Wai Shi*. By delving into explicitness/implicitness, simplification/complication, normalization/deviation, parataxis/hypotaxis, and sanitization/contamination, this research offers a multifaceted view of translation practices, contributing significantly to the field of translation studies.

4.3.2.2 The Data Collection and Analysis of Expectation Norms

The meticulous process of data collection and analysis of operational norms as previously delineated plays a pivotal role in extrapolating the expectation norms within the translation of *Ru Lin Wai Shi*. This endeavor aims to distill the essence of translation strategies into a coherent understanding of the prevailing norms. Specifically, the examination of simplification, normalization, explicitness, parataxis, and sanitization phenomena within the translated text will illuminate the inclination towards convention expectation norms. Conversely, deviations from these norms will be indicative of a foreignness expectation, suggesting a deliberate preservation of the source text's unique cultural and linguistic elements. This comprehensive analytical framework, grounded in corpus methodology, seeks not only to elucidate the nuanced translation practices employed but also to bridge a significant research gap concerning the English version of *Ru Lin Wai Shi*. By adopting this methodological approach, this chapter has meticulously laid out the research design and provided a detailed account of the research procedures, thereby setting the stage for a nuanced exploration of translation norms within this seminal work.

Chapter Five

Translation Norms in *The Scholars*

In Chapter Four, the primary research question set out to dissect the operational norms within the translation of *Ru Lin Wai Shi*, focusing specifically on whether the translation exhibited certain characteristics, including explicitness, simplification, parataxis, normalization, and sanitization, versus their counterparts—implicitness, complication, hypotaxis, and deviation. This inquiry led to an in-depth analysis of data meticulously collected from five key sources: explicitness versus implicitness, simplification versus complication, convention versus foreignness, and parataxis versus hypotaxis. The outcomes of this analysis are comprehensively presented in this chapter, culminating in the identification of the expectation norms that *The Scholars* adheres to. Moreover, the exploration extends into the second research question, which delves into the qualitative analysis to further understand the underpinning motivations and cultural considerations guiding these translation choices. This structured approach not only clarifies the operational norms but also elucidates the broader expectation norms influencing the translation strategy for *The Scholars*, offering a nuanced perspective on the translation practices employed.

5.1 The Data Collection and Analysis of Operation Norms

The objective behind delving into the operation norms within translation studies is fundamentally aimed at uncovering the underlying expectation norms that guide translational choices. Operation norms serve as a framework within which translators navigate, often manifesting distinct patterns of regularity across numerous translated texts over specific periods. These patterns are reflective of a strategic alignment with either convention or foreignness expectations, predicated on the cultural and linguistic preferences of the target audience. To accurately reconstruct and understand these operation norms, an in-depth analysis and examination of the features present in translated texts are essential. This involves a meticulous evaluation of how certain linguistic and stylistic choices conform to or deviate from the established norms, providing insights into the translator's adherence to or divergence from the expected translation practices. By systematically analyzing these features, researchers can gain a comprehensive understanding of the operation norms at play, thereby shedding light on the expectation norms that ultimately shape the translation process.

5.1.1 Simplification and Complication

Simplification and complication within translation studies present a nuanced understanding of how translators navigate the intricate balance between adhering to the source text's original complexity and adapting it to fit the linguistic and cultural context of the target audience. Simplification, as defined by Hu Kaibao in 2011, suggests that translators, perhaps subconsciously, tend to streamline the source text information to make it more accessible or understandable within the target culture. This process might involve reducing linguistic density, opting for more commonly understood words, or simplifying complex syntactic structures to facilitate easier comprehension.

On the other hand, complication in translation is characterized by a strict adherence to the original text's wording, syntactic structure, and the use of equivalent, extraordinary, or archaic words. This approach retains the source text's complex phrases and sentence patterns, preserving its original flavor and complexity at the risk of making the translation less accessible to the target audience.

The investigation into the operational norms of simplification or complication in *The Scholars* employs the standardized type/token ratio (STTR) as a key indicator for analysis. Lexical variability, or the diversity of language used in a text, serves as an indicator of whether a translation has undergone simplification or complication. A higher STTR indicates a greater variety of different, non-repeated words within a sub-corpus, reflecting a richer language variety and potentially pointing towards complication in the translation. Conversely, a lower STTR suggests a process of simplification, where language variety is reduced to make the text more digestible for the target audience.

The STTR is calculated in a standardized manner to account for variances in text lengths and to avoid data skewing. This standardization involves computing the ratio at fixed intervals, set by the researcher, across the corpus. For instance, Wordsmith Tools, a commonly used software in corpus linguistics, defaults to calculating the type/token ratio for every 1,000 words. This methodological approach ensures that the analysis remains consistent and comparable across different sections of the text or between different texts.

In the context of this study, WordSmith 7.0 was utilized to calculate the STTR for 42 chapters of *Ru Lin Wai Shi* and its English translation. This calculation aimed to quantitatively assess the degree of simplification or complication inherent in the translation, providing empirical evidence to support the analysis of operational norms. The results, presented in Table 5.1, offer a comparative view of the STTR in both the original and translated texts, shedding light on the translation strategies employed and their alignment with either simplification or complication norms. This analytical framework provides a robust basis for exploring how *The Scholars* navigates the complex terrain of translation norms, specifically in relation to simplification and complication. By examining the lexical variability and the standardized type/token ratio, this study aims to uncover the underlying expectations that guided the translation process, offering insights into the translator's approach to adapting the source text for the target audience while preserving its original complexity and nuance. Through this detailed examination, the research contributes to a deeper understanding of translation practices and the operational norms that shape them, enriching the broader discourse on translation studies.

Table 5.1 provides a revealing glimpse into the lexical diversity of *Ru Lin Wai Shi* and its English counterpart, *The Scholars*, through the lens of the standardized type/token ratio (STTR). With the STTR scores standing at 45.30 for the original Chinese text and 41.46 for the English translation, it is evident that the translation version exhibits a 3.84 point decrease in lexical variability compared to its source. This numerical distinction suggests a simplification in the language variety of the translated text. To further scrutinize this discrepancy and its implications on the translation's fidelity to the source material, an independent-samples t-test was conducted on the STTR of each chapter. This statistical analysis aims to rigorously determine whether the observed difference in STTR between *Ru Lin Wai Shi* and *The*

Scholars is statistically significant. By processing each chapter's STTR in this manner, the study endeavors to provide a quantitative foundation for understanding how simplification as an operational norm may influence the overall lexical diversity in the translation process, offering insights into the translational strategies adopted.

Table 5.1 Statistics of STTR between *Ru Lin Wai Shi* and *The Scholars*

	Ru Lin Wai Shi	***The Scholars***
Tokens	155,877	181,951
Types	10,818	8,607
TTR	6.94	4.73
STTR	45.30	41.46

Table 5.2 showcases the findings from conducting an independent-samples t-test on *Ru Lin Wai Shi* and its English version, *The Scholars*. This statistical comparison incorporates both the Levene's test for assessing variances equality and the t-test to evaluate means equality, focusing on their lexical variability. The analysis strictly adheres to established statistical benchmarks, determining the extent of lexical diversity between the original and translated works. Through this meticulous statistical evaluation, the study aims to pinpoint the differences in lexical richness, providing insights into the translational approaches regarding simplification or complication based on statistical evidence.

Table 5.2 Independent-Samples T-Test between *The Scholars* and *Ru Lin Wai Shi*

		Levene's Test for Equality of Variances		T-Test for Equality of Means			
		F	**Sig.**	***t***	***df***	**Sig. (2-tailed)**	**Mean Difference**
VAR00002	equal variances assumed	1.996	0.161	7.992	82	0.000	3.90833
	equal variances not assumed			7.992	74.496	0.000	3.90833

Interpreting the statistical outcomes presented in Table 5.2, we discern a nuanced picture of lexical variability between *Ru Lin Wai Shi* and its English translation, *The Scholars*. The application of an independent-samples *t*-test yields pivotal insights, particularly noted through the *p*-value of 0.161, which surpasses the threshold of 0.05. This initial observation suggests an absence of significant variance at this juncture. However, delving deeper into the *t*-test metrics for the first line, an intriguing statistical significance emerges, with a *t*-value of 7.992 and a *p*-value of 0.000, well below the 0.05 benchmark. This starkly signifies that the difference in the standardized type/token ratio (STTR) between the original Chinese text and its English counterpart is not merely apparent but statistically substantial.

Employed through the capabilities of Wordsmith 7.0, this analytical journey reveals a considerable reduction in lexical variability within *The Scholars* compared to *Ru Lin Wai Shi*. This finding underscores a trend towards simplification in the translation, manifest not only in lexical choice but also in mean word length and sentence structure. The translation exhibits mean word lengths and sentence lengths of 4.16 and 13.31 respectively, an indicator that, when juxtaposed against norms for professional and educated English usage—where mean sentence lengths hover around twenty to twenty-five words—suggests a discernible lean towards simplification.

This trend of simplification within *The Scholars* aligns with broader tendencies in translation practices, where the complexity inherent in the source language is often distilled to cater to the linguistic and cognitive ease of the target audience. The English version, in its effort to accommodate and resonate with its readership, arguably adopts a more accessible linguistic framework, characterized by shorter sentences and simpler vocabulary.

The Chinese language, known for its brevity and reliance on context rather than explicit linguistic markers for coherence, often features ellipsis, loose sentences, coordination, and composite sentences, lending itself naturally to shorter sentences. Lian Shuneng (2014) suggests that optimal word or sentence length in Chinese typically ranges from four to twelve characters, a standard that speaks to the language's stylistic and syntactic economy.

The translation of *Ru Lin Wai Shi* into *The Scholars*, therefore, navigates these linguistic and stylistic disparities, reflecting not only the translator's strategic choices but also the influence of the source text's inherent characteristics. Despite the broader context, topics, intended readership, purpose of writing, and stylistic preferences potentially influencing the translation, it is evident that the source text's linguistic economy has left its imprint on the translated version. This phenomenon underscores the complexity of translation as an act of balance—between fidelity to the source and the necessity of adaptation to meet the expectations and norms of the target culture.

In conclusion, the statistical analysis facilitated by Wordsmith 7.0

offers a compelling evidence base for understanding the dynamics of simplification in *The Scholars*. By quantitatively assessing the lexical variability and examining mean word and sentence lengths, this study sheds light on the nuanced ways in which *Ru Lin Wai Shi* has been transformed to align with the linguistic preferences and readability standards of its English-speaking audience. This insight not only enriches our comprehension of the specific translational strategies employed but also contributes to the broader discourse on translation norms and practices.

5.1.2 Parataxis and Hypotaxis

In the realm of linguistics, understanding the structural composition of languages involves dissecting the ways in which clauses and phrases are organized. Parataxis and hypotaxis serve as fundamental concepts in this exploration, denoting two distinct methods of arranging clauses within texts. Parataxis, as defined by Lian Shuneng (2014), involves the sequential arrangement of clauses without the use of connectives to explicitly denote their relationship, creating a structure where clauses stand in a side-by-side relation without clear hierarchical linkage. Conversely, hypotaxis is characterized by the interconnection of words or clauses through linguistic means, such as conjunctions or relative pronouns, to denote grammatical and logical relationships, thereby establishing a clear hierarchical structure within the text.

To delve deeper into the linguistic characteristics inherent in different corpora, this study employed advanced segmentation and tagging software to meticulously mark the parts of speech within each corpus. For the Chinese corpus, Corpus WordParser was utilized to segment and annotate the text, ensuring each word and phrase was accurately categorized. The English corpus underwent a similar process, employing Tokenizer, a software developed by Liang Maocheng, Li Wenzhong, and Xu Jiajin, alongside TreeTagger for Windows 3.0, to segment and tag the English text. Following this initial segmentation and annotation, the author meticulously reviewed and corrected the tagged data, ensuring a high degree of accuracy in the linguistic analysis.

With the data properly segmented and annotated, the study proceeded to employ AntConc 3.2.4, a versatile tool for corpus analysis, to calculate and analyze the linguistic composition of *Ru Lin Wai Shi*, *The Scholars*, and *Catch-22*. This analysis focused on retrieving parts of speech, including verbs, nouns, adjectives, adverbs, pronouns, prepositions, conjunctions, numerals, measure words, articles, and auxiliary words. To facilitate this, Regular Expressions (Regex) such as \S+/v for verbs, \S+/n for nouns, \S+/a for adjectives, and so forth, were used to accurately identify and categorize the various parts of speech within the texts.

The detailed examination of these linguistic elements aimed to uncover the prevalence of paratactic and hypotactic structures within the corpora, offering insights into the stylistic preferences and structural complexity of the texts. By analyzing the frequency and distribution of different parts of speech, especially focusing on conjunctions and prepositions that play pivotal roles in establishing grammatical and logical relations, the study sought to illuminate the underlying linguistic patterns that distinguish parataxis from hypotaxis in each corpus.

The culmination of this rigorous linguistic analysis is presented in Table 5.3, which showcases the findings and highlights the comparative linguistic features across the three texts. This table not only provides a quantitative basis for understanding the structural tendencies of each corpus but also offers a window into the stylistic nuances that characterize the translation practices and narrative techniques employed in *Ru Lin Wai Shi* and its English version, *The Scholars*, as well as in *Catch-22*.

Through this comprehensive linguistic exploration, the study contributes to a deeper understanding of the operational norms governing translation practices, specifically in terms of simplification, complication, and the balance between parataxis and hypotaxis. By dissecting the linguistic fabric of these texts, the research sheds light on the intricate interplay between language structure, translation strategies, and cultural nuances, enriching the discourse on translation studies and linguistic analysis.

Table 5.3 The Statistics about Parts of Speech of Different Words

Distribution Parts of Speech	*Ru Lin Wai Shi*		*The Scholars*		*Catch-22*	
	No.of Words	%	No. of Words	%	No. of Words	%
Verb	41,740	26.78	37,553	20.64	33,911	18.64
Noun	49,916	32.02	45,400	24.95	49,539	27.23
Adjective	7,329	4.70	8,943	4.92	14,393	7.91
Adverb	9,892	6.35	10,360	5.69	12,589	6.92
Pronoun	12,452	7.99	21,992	12.09	18,142	9.97
Preposition and conjunction	6,130	3.93	24,101	13.25	25,890	14.23
Numerals	5,754	3.69	2,205	1.21	1,197	0.66
Measure word	2,198	1.41	0	0	0	0
Article	0	0	14,362	7.89	12,222	6.72

Cont.

Distribution Parts of Speech	*Ru Lin Wai Shi*		*The Scholars*		*Catch-22*	
	No.of Words	%	No. of Words	%	No. of Words	%
Auxiliary word	11,425	7.33	165	0.091	91	0.051
Total number	143,859	94.90	164,916	90.73	167,883	92.33

Utilizing the data presented in Table 5.3, we leverage the analytical capabilities of Origin 7.5, a sophisticated graphing and data analysis software, to create detailed line charts depicting the distribution of parts of speech across the texts. This visualization allows us to discern the underlying trends and patterns in the linguistic structure, offering a clearer understanding of the stylistic and grammatical tendencies within the corpus.

Upon examining Figure 5.1, it becomes evident that the linguistic tendencies within *The Scholars* bear a notable resemblance to those found in original English works, diverging significantly from the patterns observed in the source text of *Ru Lin Wai Shi*. This observation suggests that the translation has been effectively adapted to align with the stylistic and grammatical conventions of the English language, making it more akin to native English compositions than to its Chinese origin. The disparity in the linguistic structure and usage between the translation of *Ru Lin Wai Shi* and its English contemporaries is markedly narrower compared to the gap between the translation and the original Chinese text. This alignment indicates a successful assimilation of the translated text into the norms and nuances of the English language, reflecting a strategic approach by the translator to render the text comprehensible and culturally resonant for English-speaking audiences.

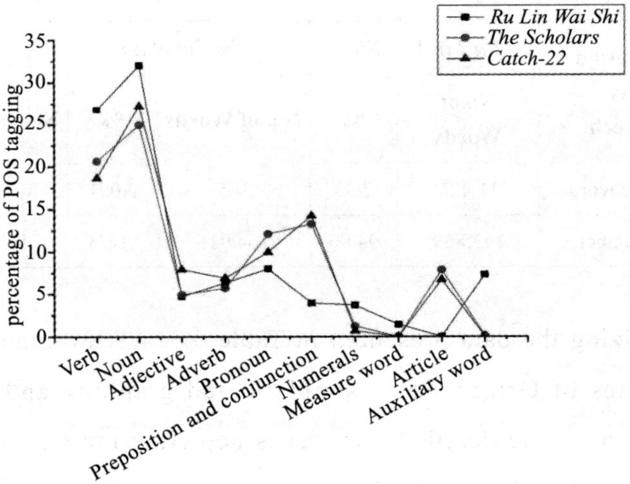

Figure 5.1 Line Charts about Distribution of Part of Speech of Three Texts

To quantify and substantiate the linguistic differences observed among the three texts—*Ru Lin Wai Shi*, its translation *The Scholars*, and representative English original works—a more rigorous statistical analysis was undertaken. The Log-Likelihood Ratio Calculator, developed by Xu Jiajin, was employed to provide a scientific basis for comparing the frequency and distribution of words across the texts. This statistical tool offers a robust method for identifying significant lexical differences, allowing for a precise measurement of the degree to which the translated text conforms to or deviates from both the source text and the established norms of English language usage.

The application of the Log-Likelihood Ratio Calculator facilitates a comprehensive examination of the lexical choices made in the translation process, illuminating how these choices contribute to the overall linguistic profile of *The Scholars*. By quantifying the similarities and differences in word usage, this analysis provides valuable insights into the translation strategies adopted, including decisions related to simplification, normalization, and the adaptation of cultural references.

The findings, as detailed in Table 5.4, reveal the specific areas where the translated text mirrors English language norms, as well as where it retains the unique linguistic features of the source text. Through this nuanced statistical treatment, the study underscores the complexity of translation as an interlingual endeavor that navigates between fidelity to the source text and the exigencies of target language expression. This balance is crucial for achieving a translation that is both faithful to the original and accessible to the target audience, ultimately contributing to a richer understanding of the translational norms that guide this intricate process.

Table 5.4 The Statistics of Log-Likelihood about Seven POS Tagging

Verb	**Log-Likelihood**	**Sig.**	**Adverb**	**Log-Likelihood**	**Sig.**
translation-original works	147.76	***+	translation-original works	242.07	***−
translation-source text	1,342.55	***−	translation-source text	59.43	***−
source text-original works	2,326.39	***+	source text-original works	52.77	***−
Noun	**Log-Likelihood**	**Sig.**	**Pronoun**	**Log-Likelihood**	**Sig.**
translation-original works	228.94	***−	translation-original works	328.73	***+
translation-source text	1,482.03	***−	translation-source text	1,407.41	***+
source text-original works	568.30	***+	source text-original works	404.72	***−

Cont.

Adjective	Log-Likelihood	Sig.	Preposition and conjunction	Log-Likelihood	Sig.
translation-original works	1,345.35	***_	translation-original works	85.24	***_
translation-source text	7.94	***+	translation-source text	8,823.88	***+
source text-original works	1,436.68	***_	source text-original works	10,444.19	***_

The analysis presented in Table 5.4 offers a comprehensive examination of linguistic differences across six categories of words between the English translation of *Ru Lin Wai Shi* and its source text, as well as between the translation and original English literary works. This detailed investigation, facilitated by the application of the Log-Likelihood Ratio Calculator, unveils significant disparities in word usage, highlighting the nuanced process of translation and its adherence to or deviation from source and target linguistic norms.

The data indicates that all six word categories exhibit pronounced differences when comparing the English translation with both the source text and original English texts. However, a noteworthy observation emerges concerning adjectives and adverbs; the Log-Likelihood Ratio Calculator for these parts of speech is lower in comparisons between the translation and original English texts than between the translation and the source text. This pattern suggests a closer alignment in the distribution of parts of speech between *The Scholars* and original English works than between the translation and *Ru Lin Wai Shi*. Such findings underscore the translation's tendency to mirror the linguistic characteristics prevalent in English literature, particularly in the usage of verbs, prepositions, and connectives, rather than strictly adhering to the syntactic and lexical patterns of the source language.

In the source text, verbs are utilized with a significantly higher frequency than in English originals, a reflection of the dynamic and action-oriented nature of Chinese narrative styles. Conversely, the English translation exhibits a moderated use of verbs, situating its frequency between the source text and English originals. This adjustment indicates a deliberate effort by the translator to balance fidelity to the source text's action-centric narrative with the stylistic preferences of English literary expression, resulting in a verb usage that, while higher than in English originals, is tempered compared to the source text.

Regarding adjectives, adverbs, prepositions, and connectives, the translation demonstrates a lower frequency compared to original English texts, suggesting a simplification or streamlining of descriptive and relational elements. However, when juxtaposed with the source text, the translation reveals a more frequent application of prepositions and connectives, deviating from the source text's less reliant use of these parts of speech to construct narrative coherence and logical relationships. This adaptation reflects the translator's navigation of linguistic structures, opting for a more explicit articulation of relationships and descriptions within the narrative to cater to English readers' expectations.

The analysis extends beyond mere frequency comparisons to delve into the implications of these linguistic shifts for cross-cultural communication and literary translation. By moderating the use of verbs and enhancing the presence of prepositions and connectives, the translation endeavors to bridge the syntactic and narrative gaps between Chinese and English storytelling traditions. This approach not only enhances the accessibility and readability of *The Scholars* for English-speaking audiences but also preserves the narrative's essence and dynamism, ensuring a faithful yet comprehensible rendition of the original text.

Moreover, the lower differences in adjectives and adverbs between the translation and original English texts, compared to those between the translation and source text, reveal a selective adaptation strategy. This strategy underscores the translator's effort to maintain the descriptive richness and adverbial nuances of the source text while aligning with the stylistic conventions of English literature.

In summary, the intricate analysis of linguistic differences, as illuminated by the Log-Likelihood Ratio Calculator, offers valuable insights into the translation strategies employed in *The Scholars*. By examining the nuanced adjustments in verbs, prepositions, connectives, adjectives, and adverbs, this study sheds light on the translator's meticulous efforts to harmonize the translated text with the linguistic and stylistic norms of English literature. Through this lens, we gain a deeper understanding of the challenges and considerations inherent in the art of literary translation, highlighting the delicate balance between fidelity to the source material and the exigencies of cross-linguistic and cross-cultural transposition.

Lian Shuneng (2014) posits a compelling distinction between English and Chinese narrative styles, describing English narrative as "static" and Chinese as "dynamic" due to its frequent use of verbs. This observation aligns with findings from our research, where numerous instances were identified that exemplify this dynamic versus static narrative dichotomy. The contrast is evident in the linguistic choices and narrative structures prevalent in the two languages, underpinning the broader stylistic tendencies that differentiate English and Chinese storytelling.

① ST: 便舍着性命去求他，及至到手之后，味同嚼蜡。

TT: Men will risk their lives in the search for them; yet once they have them within their grasp, the taste is no better than chewed tallow.

② ST: 七岁上死了父亲，他母亲做些针指供给他到村学堂里去读书。

TT: When he was seven his father died , but his mother took in sewing so that he could study at the village school.

③ ST: 第三日，杜少卿备早饭与郭孝子吃，武书也来陪着。

TT: The morning after that, Du prepared a farewell meal for Guo, at which Wu accompanied them.

④ ST: 吃罢，替他拴束了行李，拿着这二十两银子和两封书子，递与郭孝子。

TT: After the meal, they roped Guo's baggage for him and presented him with the twenty taels and two introductory letters.

⑤ ST: 马二先生见了欢喜，走进书店坐坐，取过一本来看，问个价钱，又问："这书可还行？"

TT: Ma Chunshang was delighted. He went into the shop and sat down, picked up a copy of his book and looked at it , then asked the price and how the work was selling.

In the intricate process of translating Chinese into English, a fascinating transformation occurs in the utilization of verbs and their conversion into various forms within the English language. This phenomenon is vividly demonstrated through five randomly selected examples, showcasing the dynamic nature of Chinese narrative being adapted into the more static narrative structure of English. The conversion of verbs into prepositions, prepositional phrases, or even their complete omission, reflects a profound shift in linguistic expression and narrative technique.

For instance, in the first example, the Chinese verbs "去" (go) and "求" (seek) are adeptly translated into the prepositional phrase "in the search for" in English, capturing the essence of the action while adapting it to the syntactic norms of the English language. Similarly, in the second example, the verb "到" (arrive) is replaced by the preposition "at", demonstrating a shift from an action to a state. The third example further illustrates this trend, where the verb "与" (offer) is translated into the preposition "for", altering the dynamic action into a relational state. The fourth example showcases the verb phrase "吃罢" (after eating) being substituted with "after", and "替" (for) with "for", alongside the verb "拿" (take) with "with", emphasizing the adaptation of actions into temporal or relational constructs within the English narrative.

Moreover, instances of zero replacement, where verbs are omitted entirely in the translation, underscore the differences in narrative construction between Chinese and English. Verbs like "供给" (supply), "去" (go), "读书" (study) in the second example, and verbs such as "吃" (eat), "来" (come) in the third, and "见" (see), and the second occurrence of "问" (ask) in the fifth, are omitted, simplifying the narrative structure and focusing on essential elements that align with English linguistic preferences.

The transformation of the verb phrase "做些针指" (do some sewing) in the second example into the noun "sewing" placed after an empty verb as its object, further exemplifies the shift from action-oriented to state-oriented expressions. This replacement of verbs by a significant number of prepositions, zero pronouns, and the transformation of actions into nouns represents a fundamental alteration in the way narratives are constructed and conveyed in English translations of Chinese texts.

Conjunctions in English, as noted by M.A.K. Halliday and Ruqaiya

Hasan (2001), are predicated on the linguistic system's ability to establish systematic relationships between sentences, allowing for meaningful connections within the text. In the translated text, the pervasive use of conjunctions illustrates the methods by which English narratives achieve coherence and connectivity, diverging from the more verb-centric approach of Chinese narratives.

⑥ ST: 母亲唤他到面前来说道：“儿啊，不是我有心要耽误你，只因你父亲亡后，我一个寡妇人家，只有出去的，没有进来的……”

TT:His mother called him to her and said, “Son, it's not that I want to stand in your way. But since your father died and left me a widow, I have had nothing coming in...”

⑦ ST: 马老先生，而今这银子我也不问是你出，是他出，你们原是‘毡袜裹脚靴’，但须要我效劳的来。

TT:I don't mind whether you pay the money or he pays it. Being in the same line, you're as close as sock and boot.

⑧ ST: 当下说定，约着日子来封银子。

TT:So the matter was settled, and a date fixed for the payment.

⑨ ST: 不是我说一个大胆的话：若不是我在你家，你家就一二百年也不得有个老爷走进这屋里来！

TT:I dare swear that but for the fact that I'm staying here, no gentleman would visit you even if you waited one or two hundred years!

The analysis of randomly selected examples from the translation vividly illustrates a significant linguistic transformation, particularly in the use of connectives and the conversion of parts of speech. This transformation underscores the translator's efforts to navigate between the differing narrative structures of Chinese and English, adopting strategies that align with the norms of hypotaxis and simplification. The increased incorporation of prepositions and the more frequent use of connectives in the English translation, as evidenced by an unusually high log-likelihood ratio, suggest a deliberate effort to enhance the clarity of logical relationships and grammatical connections within the text. This adjustment results in a translated narrative where conjunctions and prepositions are utilized more extensively than in the original source text, reflecting a shift towards making the logical relations between sentences or phrases more explicit.

This adaptation is indicative of a broader strategy to conform to the expectations of English readers, who may require more explicit markers of logical and grammatical relationships due to the syntactic differences between English and Chinese. By adding functional words such as prepositions and connectives, the translation seeks to bridge these structural gaps, ensuring that the narrative flow and coherence are maintained in a manner that resonates with the target language audience.

Moreover, the data presented in the analysis reveals a notable discrepancy in the frequency of nouns and pronouns between the source text and its English translation. Specifically, the frequency of nouns in the translation is significantly lower than in the source text, whereas the use of pronouns is markedly higher. This observation suggests that the translation process may involve substitutions of nouns with pronouns or the addition of pronouns to maintain narrative continuity and cohesion. Such linguistic choices could be driven by the need to adapt the text to the stylistic and grammatical conventions of English, where pronouns often play a crucial role in ensuring clarity and avoiding repetition.

The presence of these substitutions and additions is further corroborated by numerous instances identified throughout the research. For example, where the source text might rely on nouns to convey meaning, the English translation often opts for pronouns to maintain the narrative flow and ensure coherence across sentences. This strategy not only aligns with the simplification norm by reducing the complexity of noun phrases but also adheres to the hypotactic structure of English by using pronouns to clearly indicate relationships between different parts of the text.

The examples analyzed in this study highlight the translator's nuanced understanding of both the source and target languages, demonstrating a sophisticated approach to bridging linguistic and cultural divides. By carefully adjusting the use of nouns and pronouns and incorporating a higher frequency of connectives and prepositions, the translation effectively negotiates the stylistic preferences and expectations of English readers. This linguistic adaptation reflects a deep engagement with the operation norms of hypotaxis and simplification, showcasing the translator's skill in rendering a text that is not only faithful to the original but also accessible and coherent to the target audience.

In summary, the detailed examination of linguistic transformations in the translation of *Ru Lin Wai Shi* into English reveals a complex interplay of narrative strategies, grammatical adjustments, and stylistic considerations. Through the strategic use of pronouns, prepositions, and connectives, the translation navigates the structural and stylistic differences between Chinese and English, embodying a careful balance between fidelity to the source text and adherence to the linguistic norms of the target language. This analysis underscores the translator's role as a mediator between cultures, highlighting the intricate decisions that underpin the translation process and contribute to the creation of a text that resonates with readers across linguistic boundaries.

(1)Nominal substitution

⑩ ST: 屠户连忙把拳头缩了回去，往腰里揣，口里说道：“也罢，你而今相与了这个张老爷，何愁没有银子用？他家里的银子，说起来比皇帝家还多些哩！他家就是我卖肉的主顾，一年就是无事，肉也要用四五千斤，银子何足为奇!”

TT:Butcher Hu immediately drew back his fist, stuffed the silver into his pocket and said," All right. Now that you are on good terms with that Mr. Zhang, you needn't be afraid of going short. His family has more silver than the emperor, and they are my best customers. Every year, even if they have no particular occasions to celebrate, they still buy four or five thousand catties of meat. Silver is nothing to him.

⑪ ST: 当下携了马二先生的手，走出丁仙祠，却是一条平坦大路，一块石头也没有。未及一刻功夫，已到了伍相国庙门口。

TT:Taking Ma Chunshang's hand, this stranger led him out of the temple to a wide flat road on which there was not a single stone, and in next to no time they had reached the temple of Wu Zixu.

⑫ ST: 这书刻出来，封面上就刻先生的名号，还多寡有几两选金和几十本样书送与先生。

TT:We shall print your name on the title page, and when the book comes out you will receive a few dozen copies as well as several taels of silver.

In the exploration of translation strategies employed in converting *Ru Lin Wai Shi* to its English counterpart, *The Scholars*, a striking observation emerges from Example ⑩, where the phrase “ 他家 ” is adeptly translated into the pronoun “they”. This substitution not only simplifies the narrative but also leads to a reduction in the use of specific nouns, as evidenced by the omission of words like "口里" (in the mouth) and "肉" (meat) in the English rendition. Such ellipses are indicative of a strategic choice to streamline the narrative by reducing noun density, thereby enhancing readability and coherence for English readers.

Similarly, in Example ⑫, the term "先生" is translated as "you", demonstrating a further conversion from a noun to a pronoun, which personalizes and simplifies the narrative flow. Additionally, the omission of "门口" (at the door) in Example ⑪ highlights a consistent application of ellipsis as a translation technique. These instances of word class conversion and strategic omission contribute significantly to the overall reduction of nouns in the translated text.

This approach to translation reflects a nuanced understanding of the target language's stylistic preferences, where the use of pronouns can often provide a more fluid and engaging narrative experience compared to the more noun-heavy structure typical of Chinese. By employing these techniques, the translator effectively bridges the linguistic and cultural gap between the source and target texts, ensuring that the essence of the original narrative is preserved while adapting its form to meet the expectations of English-speaking audiences.

(2) Adding pronouns

⑬ ST: 众人七手八脚将他扛抬了出来，贡院前一个茶棚子里坐下，劝他吃了一碗茶，犹自索鼻涕，弹眼泪，伤心不止。

TT: Then all the others lent a hand to carry him out and set him down in a tea-house in front of the examination school. They urged him to drink a bow of tea. But he just went on sniffing and blinking away his tears, looking quite broken-hearted.

⑭ ST: 出衙门，同差人坐在一个茶馆里吃了一壶茶，起身又要走。

TT:He went out of the yamen with the runner, and they sat down in a tea-house to drink a pot of tea. Then Yu stood up to go.

⑮ ST: 只见那戏子都已散了，施御史也回去了，只有高翰林还在这里等信，看见凤四老爹回来，忙问道："到底为甚事?"

TT:The players had left, and so had Censor Shi, but Gao was still waiting for news. "What actually happened?" he asked the moment Feng came in.

⑯ ST: 沈琼枝自从来到南京，挂了招牌，也有来求诗的，也有来买斗方的，也有来托刺绣的。

TT:Since arriving in Nanjing and hanging up her signboard, customers had come to her to order poems, calligraphy and embroidery.

⑰ ST: 你问这个人怎的？莫不是那家要娶他？这个堂客是娶不得的！若娶进门，就要一把天火!"

TT:Why do you ask about her? Surely nobody is thinking of marrying her, is he? The woman is quite impossible. Any man who marries her will be taking a fury into his house.

The nuanced process of translating from Chinese to English involves more than mere linguistic conversion; it encompasses adapting narrative techniques to suit the linguistic and cultural context of the target audience. A closer examination of the examples provided reveals a strategic augmentation of the English translation with pronouns that were only implied in the original Chinese text, thereby enhancing clarity and coherence for English readers.

In Example ⑬, the addition of the pronouns "him" and "they" explicitly identifies Zhou Jin and others present in the examination hall, persons who, in the source text, might have been referred to more obliquely. This practice of adding corresponding pronouns is consistently observed across Examples ⑭ ⑮ and ⑯, where the translators have meticulously inserted pronouns to clarify references to individuals that were not explicitly mentioned in the source text. Similarly, Example ⑰ showcases a generalization in the use of the third-person singular pronouns for both men and women with the word "he", a usage that could potentially obscure the specific gender being referred to. To mitigate this ambiguity, the personal pronoun "her" is introduced in the translation, serving to clarify the vague logical relationships inherent in the original narrative.

This translation strategy reflects a fundamental difference in narrative style and pronoun usage between Chinese and English. Lian Shuneng (2014) notes that Chinese tends to utilize real names rather than pronouns, resulting in less frequent pronoun use compared to English and other European languages. However, to avoid repetition and maintain narrative consistency, English translations often resort to the extensive use of personal pronouns. Furthermore, the integration of relative words, conjunctions, and prepositions in English serves to articulate the logical relationships between sentences and clauses more explicitly.

The deliberate addition of pronouns in the English version of *Ru Lin Wai Shi* exemplifies the translators' commitment to achieving clarity and fluency in the translated text. This approach not only aligns with the simplification norm—streamlining the narrative to enhance its readability—but also underscores the principle of explicitness, ensuring that the relationships between characters and their actions are clearly understood by the target audience.

Moreover, the translators' decision to add pronouns and clarify references reflects a deep engagement with the source material, demonstrating an effort to preserve the narrative's integrity while adapting it to the linguistic preferences of English readers. By addressing the implicitness of pronouns in the original Chinese text, the translation navigates the cultural and linguistic nuances of pronoun usage, facilitating a more accessible and engaging narrative experience for English-speaking audiences.

In sum, the translation of *Ru Lin Wai Shi* into English illustrates the complex interplay between fidelity to the source text and the norms of the target language. The translators' strategic use of pronouns and other linguistic devices to clarify and enhance the narrative demonstrates a sophisticated understanding of both languages' narrative structures. Through this meticulous process, the translation achieves a balance between maintaining the essence of the original story and ensuring its resonance with English-speaking readers, highlighting the artistry and thoughtfulness inherent in the craft of translation.

5.1.3 Normalization and Deviation

Normalization within the realm of translation is a concept that delves into how the inherent textual relationships in the source material often undergo modifications to align more closely with the habitual linguistic patterns present in the target language's repertoire. Gideon Toury (1995) articulates this notion, suggesting that translations tend to gravitate towards conforming to the conventional expressions and structures of the target language, often at the expense of the original text's more innovative or unique linguistic elements. This inclination towards normalization is driven by a desire to make the translated text resonate with the target audience by adhering to their linguistic expectations and norms.

Conversely, deviation in translation encapsulates the deliberate effort to preserve the distinctiveness of the source text. This approach involves consciously choosing to retain the original's unique expressions, specialized terminology, and even instances of perceived errors or logical inconsistencies. By embracing deviation, translators allow the target language readers to experience the peculiarities and idiosyncrasies of the source language, fostering a deeper engagement with the original cultural and linguistic context.

The exploration of whether a translated text leans towards normalization or deviation is particularly pertinent when examining the treatment of Chinese idioms in translation. Chinese idioms, with their rich cultural significance and compact linguistic expression, pose a unique challenge in translation. These idioms encompass a variety of forms, including two-part allegorical sayings, proverbs, colloquialisms, and set phrases, each carrying nuanced meanings and historical connotations.

To undertake a detailed study of how Chinese idioms are translated, it is essential first to identify and categorize the idioms present in the *Ru Lin Wai Shi* corpus. Following the categorization proposed by Feng Jie (2016), idioms are marked according to their specific types: "X" for two-part allegorical sayings, "S" for colloquialisms, "Y" for proverbs, and "G" for set phrases. This classification allows for a systematic approach to analyzing how each type of idiom is rendered in the translation.

Employing PowerGREP 4, a powerful search and extraction tool, the research extracts all instances of these idiomatic expressions from the corpus, setting the stage for an in-depth analysis of their translation. This process involves scrutinizing how the idioms are translated and determining whether the translations exhibit tendencies towards normalization—adopting more conventional expressions that align with the target language's norms—or deviation, wherein the unique aspects of the idioms are preserved to maintain their cultural and linguistic specificity.

The analysis of idiomatic translation is not merely a linguistic exercise but also a cultural exploration. It reveals the translator's strategies in navigating between the source and target languages, illuminating the choices made to either integrate the text seamlessly into the target language context or to highlight its foreign origins. This balance between normalization and deviation is crucial in determining how the translated text bridges cultural divides, offering insights into the translator's role as a mediator between languages and cultures.

In essence, the study of Chinese idioms' translation characteristics within *Ru Lin Wai Shi* serves as a microcosm of the broader dynamics at play in translation studies. It reflects the ongoing dialogue between fidelity to the source text and adaptability to the target language, showcasing the intricate decision-making process that underpins the translation of culturally and linguistically rich texts. Through this analysis, we gain a deeper understanding of the complexity involved in translating Chinese idioms and the implications of these choices for cross-cultural communication and literary translation.

(1) Two-part allegorical sayings

The two-part allegorical saying, a unique and intricate form of Chinese idiomatic expression, is characterized by its division into two distinct components: the quoting part and the annotating part. This structural bifurcation stands as the hallmark feature that sets it apart from other forms of idioms within the rich tapestry of Chinese linguistic traditions, as elucidated by Feng Jie (2016). The quoting part typically presents an historical reference or a piece of conventional wisdom, encapsulating it in a succinct and often metaphorical phrase. The annotating part then follows, providing explanation or commentary that unravels the deeper meaning or moral lesson embedded within the quoted phrase. This dual-structured idiom not only conveys literal information but also imparts profound insights, embodying the wisdom and cultural nuances of Chinese heritage. The translation of such two-part allegorical sayings poses a significant challenge, requiring the translator to adeptly navigate the nuances of both parts to preserve the idiomatic expression's integrity and depth in another linguistic and cultural context.

⑱ ST: 我说二三百银子，你就说二三十两，<X>‘戴着斗笠亲嘴，差着一帽子！’

TT: When I say two or three hundred taels, you say twenty or thirty! It's like kissing in straw helmets—the lips are far apart!

The two-part allegorical saying, "戴着斗笠亲嘴，差着一帽子," serves as a vivid illustration of the runner's greed and acerbity, encapsulating complex human behaviors through a simple, yet profound, metaphorical expression. This saying, rich in imagery and cultural nuance, highlights the subtlety and depth of Chinese idiomatic expressions. The Yangs, in their translation work, faced the challenge of rendering this idiom into English in a way that both preserves its original form and ensures it resonates with an English-speaking audience.

In tackling this particular two-part allegorical saying, the Yangs opted to maintain the structural integrity of the saying, thereby honoring its original form. This approach underscores their commitment to retaining the cultural and linguistic essence of the source text. However, recognizing the potential difficulties English readers might encounter in directly deciphering the metaphorical and cultural references embedded in the second part of the saying, the Yangs employed a strategy of normalization for its translation.

This normalized translation strategy involved rephrasing or explaining the second part of the saying in terms that are more familiar and accessible to the target audience, thereby enhancing readability without diluting the saying's intended meaning. By adopting this method, the Yangs skillfully bridged the cultural and linguistic gap between the original Chinese text and its English rendition, ensuring that the allegorical saying's critique of greed and acerbity is clearly conveyed and appreciated by readers unfamiliar with the original cultural context.

⑲ ST:<X>'猪八戒吃人参果，全不知滋味'！说的好容易！

TT: You had no business touching it, you scoundrel!

This proverbial saying, originating from the classic Chinese literature *Journey to the West*, has evolved beyond its literary roots to metaphorically describe individuals who are so consumed by greed that they fail to appreciate the sustenance they have consumed. In their English translation of the text, the Yangs chose to omit this saying, a decision that underscores the challenges inherent in translating culturally specific idioms. This omission reflects a translation strategy that may prioritize narrative flow and reader comprehension over direct linguistic equivalence, particularly when dealing with expressions deeply rooted in cultural lore and historical context.

⑳ ST: 方才这几片，不要说值几十两银子，<X>'半夜里不见了枪头子——攮到贼肚里'；只是我将来再发了晕病，却拿甚么药来医？

TT:Nearly a hundred tael's worth of medicine has disappeared down your throat! And what am I to take next time I have an attack?

This particular saying, originally crafted to denounce those who clandestinely consume food, has been nuancedly translated by the Yangs into English, where only its essence—"disappear down your throat"—is retained, with the vivid imagery and allegorical layers stripped away. This reduction to the core idea serves to simplify and clarify the intended message for English readers, albeit at the expense of the rich metaphorical context that characterizes the original Chinese expression. In the narrative context, this saying is wielded by Yan to satirize the steersman, a surface interpretation that masks the deeper intention of the author, Wu Jingzi. Through the original saying, Wu Jingzi sought to cast Yan's acridness and morally repugnant nature in a sharply witty tone, employing the allegorical saying as a literary device to reveal character flaws.

However, in the Yangs' translation, while the underlying message of the source text is preserved and made accessible, the omission of the allegorical imagery results in a dilution of the original's sarcastic bite. This approach, aimed at producing an idiomatic and "readable" target text, underscores the translation challenges of balancing fidelity to the source material with the need for clarity and fluency in the target language. The translated version, therefore, while effective in conveying the core meaning, falls short of fully capturing the nuanced satire and the rich cultural connotations embedded in Wu Jingzi's original narrative, highlighting the complexity involved in translating culturally and linguistically dense expressions.

Additional examples of normalized translations for two-part allegorical sayings are provided below:

㉑ ST: 周进听了这话，自己想：<X> "'瘫子掉在井里，捞起来也是坐。' 有甚亏负我？"

TT:"Even if a paralytic falls into a well, he can be no worse off than before," thought Zhou Jin." It can't hurt me to go."

㉒ ST: 怪不得人说你们'诗云子曰'的人难讲话。这样看来，你好像 <X>'老鼠尾巴上害疖子，出脓也不多'！

TT:No wonder they say you bookworms are hard to deal with:one might just as well try to squeeze water out of a stone.

㉓ ST: 同你共事，你是 <X>'马蹄刀瓢里切菜，滴水也不漏'，总不肯放出钱来。

TT:I've never worked with anyone so close-fisted. You can't bear parting with a cent!

Below are further examples of translations that exhibit deviation for two-part allegorical sayings:

㉔ ST: 姑奶奶平日只敬重的王家哥儿两个，把我们不睬不睬，我们没来由今日为他得罪严老大，<X>'老虎头上扑苍蝇'怎的？

TT:She always thought so highly of those Wang brothers, and treated us like dirt. Why should we offend Senior Licentiate Yan for her sake? Only fools catch flies on a tiger's head.

㉕ ST: 真是 <X> 哑子梦见妈，说不出来的苦！

TT:Now, like a dumb man dreaming of his mother, he could not express his despair!

Other ellipses about two-part allegorical saying are listed as follows:

㉖ ST: 瞎子听了半天，听他两人说的都是 <X>"堂屋里挂草荐，不是话"，也就不扯劝，慢慢的摸着回去了。

TT:After hearing all the nonsense they were talking, the blind man gave up trying to reason with them and groped his way back to his room.

In conclusion, the English translations of two-part allegorical sayings are presented in Table 5.5 below:

Table 5.5 The English Translation about Two-Part Allegorical Sayings in *The Scholars*

Type of Translation	Frequency	Ratio
normalization	5	56%
deviation	2	22%
ellipsis	2	22%
in total	9	100%

Observations from Table 5.5 reveal that instances of deviation in the translated text are comparatively few, indicating a predominant inclination towards normalization within the version. This pattern suggests that the translation approach for two-part allegorical sayings in *The Scholars* predominantly aligns with the norms and conventions of the target language, thus categorizing the translation strategy as relatively normalized. This adherence to normalization underscores the translators' intent to ensure the translated text's accessibility and comprehensibility for the target audience, effectively adapting the original idiomatic expressions into forms more familiar to English readers.

(2) Colloquialisms

Colloquialisms, as encountered in *The Scholars*, are intricately designed with two distinct layers of interpretation: the surface or literal meaning, and a deeper, often concealed meaning. The language employed within these colloquial expressions typically carries stylistic nuances that tend to skew towards the informal or even derogatory, reflecting the social attitudes or character insights intended by the author. These colloquialisms serve not only as linguistic devices but also as cultural markers, offering insights into the societal norms and values embedded within the narrative context. The specific colloquialisms identified in *The Scholars* are meticulously cataloged in the subsequent table, showcasing the range and depth of such expressions utilized throughout the text to enrich the storytelling with authentic dialogue and nuanced character portrayals.

Analysis of Table 5.6 reveals a noteworthy pattern: instances of normalization within the translated text are relatively few, illustrating a clear inclination towards deviation in the translation strategy employed. This trend indicates that the approach to translating colloquialisms in *The Scholars* favors retaining the unique cultural and linguistic nuances of the original expressions over conforming to the target language's norms. Consequently, the translation strategy for colloquialisms in the text can be characterized as predominantly deviating, aiming to preserve the authenticity and richness of the source material's vernacular speech.

Table 5.6 The English Translation about Colloquialisms in *The Scholars*

Type of Translation	Source Text	Translated Text	Frequency	Ratio
deviated translation	<S> 癞蛤蟆想吃起天鹅肉	...you're like a toad trying to swallow a swan!	13	56.52%
	<S> 白刀子进去，红刀子出来	Every day the blade goes in white and comes out red.		
	<S> 撒泡尿自己照照	...piss on the ground and look at your face in the puddle!		
	<S> 娃子不哭奶不胀	If the baby doesn't cry, the milk doesn't flow.		
	为甚么 <S> 把别人家的棺材拉在自己门口哭？	Why lug someone else's coffin to your door and cry over it?		

Cont.

Type of Translation	Source Text	Translated Text	Frequency	Ratio
deviated translation	<S> 三十年河东，三十年河西	...for thirty years people east of the river prosper, then for thirty years those on the west.	13	56.52%
	<S> 秀才人情纸半张	Scholars express their friendship on paper.		
	<S> 天下何人不识君？	Is there anyone who does not know you?		
	<S> 死知府不如一个活老鼠	A dead prefect is not as good as a live rat.		
	<S> 滚水泼老鼠	...like a rat in scalding water...		
	<S> 躲得和尚躲不得寺	The runaway monk can't run away with the temple.		
	<S> 沉鱼落雁之容，闭月羞花之貌	...her beauty would put the flowers to shame.		
	<S> 赔了夫人又折兵	You've lost the campaign and your wife into the bargain!		
normalized translation	<S>'陈猫古老鼠'的文章	...wrote essays in an outmoded style...	10	43.48%
	<S> 开弓不放箭	...to try a little blackmail...		
	<S>'稂不稂莠不莠'的到几时?	How long can you go on like this—neither fish, flesh nor fowl?		
	<S> 没脊骨钻狗洞	...is going to bad places...		
	<S> 打开板壁讲亮话	Let's be frank and put all our cards on the table...		
	<S> 一点水一个泡	I always stick strictly to the truth...		

Cont.

Type of Translation	Source Text	Translated Text	Frequency	Ratio
normalized translation	<S> 地头文书铁箍桶	...the established procedure has always been to consider the local verdict as cast-iron evidence.	10	43.48%
	<S> 晚娘的拳头，云里的日头	A stepmother is always cruel.		
	<S> 世情看冷暖，人面逐高低	Warm feelings may turn to coldness. Men are drawn to prosperity but not to adversity.		
	<S> 过了庙不下雨	...forget to thank me...		
total number			23	100%

(3) Proverbs

Proverbs are traditionally recognized for their role in disseminating knowledge, serving as the core and distinctive feature that sets them apart. Within *The Scholars*, such proverbs are meticulously compiled and showcased, offering a glimpse into the wisdom they encapsulate. These are systematically laid out in the subsequent table for detailed examination and appreciation.

A close examination of Table 5.7 reveals that instances of normalization within the translated text of *Ru Lin Wai Shi* are comparatively scarce. This observation underscores a predominant trend towards deviation in the translation approach adopted for the text. Consequently, it can be inferred that the methodology applied to the translation of proverbs in *The Scholars* leans significantly towards preserving the original's idiosyncratic features, thereby categorizing the translation's overall direction as notably deviated from conventional expressions.

Table 5.7 The English translation about Proverbs in *The Scholars*

Type of Translation	Source Text	Translated Text	Frequency	Ratio
normalized translation	<Y> 人逢喜事精神爽	Joy puts heart into a man.	9	36%
	<Y> 龙头属老成	First-class honours go to the mature...		
	<Y> 三十六计，走为上计	Better make myself scarce...		
	<Y> 河水不洗船	I don't like seeing any man ruined.		
	<Y> 打蛇打七寸	...you've got to act quickly in this...		
	<Y> 君子成人之美	A friend in need is a friend indeed!		
	<Y> 名不正则言不顺	You must conform to etiquette.		
	<Y> 夫妻无隔宿之仇	Nothing can come between husband and wife.		
	<Y> 瞒天讨价，就地还钱	This is just like the proverb: The price is as high as the sky and the offer as low as the earth...		
deviated translation	<Y> 好男不吃分家饭，好女不穿嫁时衣	Good sons don't live on their inheritance; good daughters don't wear clothes from their own homes after they marry.	16	64%
	<Y> 公而忘私，国而忘家	Public business comes before private affairs. The state comes before the family.		

Cont.

Type of Translation	Source Text	Translated Text	Frequency	Ratio
deviated translation	<Y> 处则不失为真儒，出则可以为王佐	In retirement he would be a great scholar; and in office he could be the councillor of kings.	16	64%
	<Y> 蜂虿入怀，解衣去赶	...if a wasp gets next to your skin, remove your coat to shake it off.		
	<Y> 书中自有黄金屋，书中自有千钟粟，书中自有颜如玉	There are golden mansions in study; there are bushels of rice and beautiful women.		
	<Y> 一斗米养个恩人，一石米养个仇人	A peck of rice wins you a friend; a bushel wins you a foe.		
	<Y> 公门里好修行	The yamen is a good place to do good deeds.		
	<Y> 清官难断家务事	Officials can't interfere in family disputes...		
	<Y> 见义不为，是为无勇	A man who knows what is the right thing to do, but doesn't do it, is a coward!		
	<Y> 人在画图中	In a beautiful scene a man feels he is part of a picture.		
	<Y> 灭门的知县	Magistrates can ruin families.		
	<Y> 无兵无粮，因甚不降？	No troops, no food, why not surrender?		
	<Y> 作文之心如人目	In writing an essay the mind should remain as clear as the human eye.		
	<Y> 如入宝山空手回	Isn't that like going to a treasure-trove and coming away empty-handed?		

Cont.

Type of Translation	Source Text	Translated Text	Frequency	Ratio
deviated translation	<Y> 钱到公事办，火到猪头烂	Fire cooks pork and money works wonders.	16	64%
	<Y> 相交满天下，知心能几人	...a man may have acquaintances all over the world, but very few true friends.		
total number			25	100%

(4) Set phrases

Set phrases typically consist of four characters, as demonstrated by the following examples:

㉗ ST: 这位小姐德性温良，才貌出众，鲁老先生和夫人因无子息，爱如 <G> 掌上之珠，许多人家求亲，只是不允。

TT: ...and she is virtuous, gentle and beautiful. Because Mr. and Mrs. Lu have no son, this girl is the apple of their eye; so although many families have sought her hand in marriage, her parents would never consent.

The Chinese set phrase "掌上之珠," also referred to as "掌上明珠," encapsulates the profound affection parents hold for their daughter, likening her to a precious pearl resting in the palm of their hand. This vivid imagery serves not only as a testament to the value and adoration bestowed upon the child but also reflects the cultural significance of expressing familial love and cherishment in Chinese society. The metaphor of a pearl, universally recognized for its beauty and rarity, aptly symbolizes the uniqueness and preciousness of a beloved daughter within the family unit, highlighting her as a source of pride and joy.

In parallel, the idiom "the apple of one's eye," with its origins traced back to the Bible, carries a similar connotation in the English language. Contrary to the initial assumption that "apple" might refer to the fruit, it actually denotes the "pupil" of the eye, underscoring the notion of something or someone being deeply cherished and regarded as invaluable. The pupil, being central to the eye's function and thus pivotal for vision, is metaphorically employed to convey the idea of holding someone in the highest esteem, akin to safeguarding the most critical and precious part of one's being.

The English idiom extends beyond the scope of familial affection to encompass a broader range of precious entities or beloved individuals. Its versatility allows for its application in various contexts where the intent is to express profound appreciation, love, or irreplaceability. Despite these differences in applicability and cultural origins, when utilized to describe Miss Lu in *The Scholars*, both idioms — "掌上之珠" and "the apple of one's eye" — converge in function and significance. They effectively convey the narrative's portrayal of Miss Lu as the cherished daughter of the Lu family, embodying her paramount importance and the deep affection she commands.

This convergence of meaning between the two idioms from distinct cultural backgrounds underscores the universality of certain human emotions and values, particularly the love and esteem for family members. In the context of *The Scholars*, the choice of "the apple of one's eye" as a conventional translation for "掌上之珠" bridges linguistic and cultural gaps, ensuring that the essence of the expression — the profound parental love for a daughter — is preserved and resonates with English-speaking audiences. Thus, despite the broader applicability of the English idiom, its use in this specific context mirrors the original sentiment of the Chinese phrase, highlighting the beloved status of Miss Lu within her family and by extension, within the narrative.

㉘ ST: 初时撑着，每晚算账，直算到三更鼓，后来就渐渐饮食不进，<G> 骨瘦如柴，又舍不得银子吃人参。

TT: At first he just put up with them, doing his accounts as usual every night until mid-night; but gradually he lost his appetite and wasted away till he was nothing but skin and bones. Yet he grudged the money to buy ginseng.

The Chinese idiom "骨瘦如柴," which vividly describes a person's extreme thinness, akin to being as slender as a stick or lath, presents a linguistic and cultural challenge in translation. The Yangs, in their translation endeavor, adeptly selected the English idiomatic expression "skin and bones" to encapsulate the essence of "骨瘦如柴." This choice is particularly noteworthy for its naturalness and simplicity, ensuring that the target readership gains an immediate and accurate comprehension of the imagery and meaning originally conveyed in the source text.

The phrase "skin and bones" in English serves as a direct, functional equivalent to the Chinese idiom, effectively communicating the visual and emotional impact of someone's emaciated condition. This translation not only preserves the vividness of the description but also maintains the idiomatic flavor, allowing English readers to access the cultural and emotional nuances embedded in the original expression. The decision to employ an existing English idiom with a parallel function and imagery underscores a strategic approach to translation that prioritizes idiomatic and functional equivalence, thereby facilitating a cross-cultural transfer of meaning and sentiment.

In instances such as this, the direct borrowing of English idioms to translate analogous Chinese expressions achieves a remarkable level of functional equivalence in the target language. Given their inherent idiomatic nature in English, these expressions enable target readers to fully engage with and appreciate the text in a manner that closely mirrors the experience of the source language readers. This approach not only enhances the readability and relatability of the translated text but also fosters a deeper intercultural understanding by bridging linguistic and conceptual gaps between the source and target languages.

Moreover, the use of "skin and bones" in place of "骨瘦如柴" exemplifies the translators' sensitivity to the target audience's linguistic expectations and cultural perceptions. By selecting idioms that resonate with English-speaking readers, the translators ensure that the descriptive power and emotional resonance of the original text are not lost in translation. This careful consideration of both the linguistic and cultural dimensions of translation highlights the complexity of the translators' task and their commitment to achieving a translation that is both faithful to the original and accessible to the new audience.

Ultimately, the translation of "骨瘦如柴" into "skin and bones" represents a successful endeavor to maintain the expressive depth and cultural richness of the source text while making it comprehensible and engaging for English readers. This strategy underscores the importance of idiomatic expressions in capturing the essence of the original language and culture, demonstrating the translators' adeptness at navigating the intricate process of cultural adaptation and linguistic transformation.

㉙ ST: 席终，归到新房里，重新摆酒，夫妻 <G> 举案齐眉。

TT: After this he returned to his chamber, where wine was served again and husband and wife feasted together.

"举案齐眉" is an allusion to describe a happy marriage. It tells a story of Liang Hong and his wife Meng Guang in the Han Dynasty. Every time when Liang came home, Meng offered the dishes to him respectfully in the way of holding the plate to the place of her eyebrow. Liang also accepted it in a courteous way. Later on, the allusion is widely used to show that "a married couple love and respect each other for life." All the information is condensed into four Chinese characters. As to the English version the cultural information is lost in order to send an easier understanding.

㉚ ST: 幸得衙门后身紧靠着北城，几个衙役先溜到城外，用绳子把张、范二位系了出去，换了蓝布衣服，草帽草鞋，寻一条小路，忙忙如 <G> 丧家之狗，急急如 <G> 漏网之鱼，连夜找路回省城去了。

TT: Luckily, the back of the yamen was hard by the north gate of the city, and after several men had slipped outside the city wall, Mr. Zhang and Fan Jin were lowered to them by ropes. Then Zhang and Fan changed into blue cloth gowns, straw hats and sandals, and, stealthily as stray dogs, swiftly as fish escaping from the net, fled back to the provincial capital.

The translation of "丧家之狗" and "漏网之鱼" into "stray dogs" and "fish escaping from the net" respectively, exemplifies a deviation from a straightforward linguistic conversion to a more culturally nuanced interpretation in the English version of the text. The choice to render "丧家之狗" as "stealthily as stray dogs" in English demonstrates a deliberate effort to preserve the imagery and connotations associated with the term "狗" (dog) from the original Chinese context. This translation choice is particularly significant given the contrasting cultural perceptions surrounding dogs in Chinese and Western societies.

In Chinese culture, the term “狗” (dog) is rarely used in a commendatory manner; it often carries negative connotations, reflecting social disdain or pity. The phrase “丧家之狗” is imbued with this cultural specificity, and its meaning goes far beyond the literal description of a dog without a home, suggesting a sense of loss, displacement, or disgrace. In contrast, Western culture holds a more favorable view of dogs, frequently associating them with loyalty, companionship, and valor. Thus, the translation of “丧家之狗” into “stray dogs” introduces an element of cultural strangeness to the target audience, challenging them to reconcile the familiar image of dogs with the more disparaging implications rooted in the source text.

Similarly, the translation of “漏网之鱼” as “fish escaping from the net” captures the essence of narrow escape and freedom inherent in the original expression while maintaining the aquatic imagery. However, the transformation of this idiom into a more descriptive phrase in English seeks to make the concept immediately accessible to readers unfamiliar with the Chinese idiom’s cultural background. By doing so, the translation navigates the delicate balance between preserving the source text’s imagery and ensuring that the metaphor resonates within the target cultural context.

These examples of deviated translation underscore the translators’ nuanced approach to bridging cultural differences through the adaptation of idiomatic expressions. By carefully selecting terms that both reflect the original imagery and align with the target audience’s cultural expectations, the translators facilitate a deeper engagement with the text. This strategy highlights the complex interplay between fidelity to the source material and the need to render the translation meaningful and relatable to the target audience, underscoring the intricate challenges and considerations that inform the translation process.

㉛ ST: 那人道："久仰大名，<G> 如雷灌耳，只是无缘，不曾拜识。"

TT: "Your fame, which resounds like thunder, has long since reached my ears," said the stranger."But hitherto I have had no opportunity of making your acquaintance."

The Chinese idiom "如雷灌耳," which is utilized to depict someone's immense reputation or fame, showcases the vivid imagery of thunder ("雷") piercing through the ears ("耳"), evoking a sense of widespread and impactful recognition. In the translation process, the decision to render the original images of "雷" (thunder) and "耳" (ears) literally into English, though it might appear unconventional or peculiar to English readers, strategically preserves the essence and intensity of the metaphor. This literal translation approach ensures that the core message of the source text — the extent and force of an individual's renown — is effectively communicated to the target audience without leading to confusion or inappropriate connotations. Despite the potential for cultural strangeness due to the direct rendering of these images, the translation succeeds in conveying the idiom's meaning, demonstrating that the resonance of the original expression's power and immediacy is maintained, allowing English readers to grasp the significance of being so well-known that one's reputation resounds like thunder, clearly and unambiguously.

The statistical analysis of additional set phrase translations within *The Scholars* is detailed in the table below:

Table 5.8 The Statistic of the English Translation about Set Phrases in *The Scholars*

Type of Translation	Frequency	Ratio
normalized translation	50	66%
deviated translation	23	30%
ellipsis	3	4%
in total	76	100%

Analyzing Table 5.8 provides insightful observations regarding the translation strategies employed in *The Scholars*. It becomes evident that occurrences of deviation from the source text's original expressions are minimal within the translated text. This pattern suggests a pronounced inclination towards normalization, where the translators have opted for rendering the idiomatic expressions in a manner that aligns more closely with the linguistic norms and cultural expectations of the target audience. Such an approach indicates that the translation of proverbs in *The Scholars* predominantly adheres to a strategy of normalization, prioritizing readability and comprehension for English readers over strict adherence to the source text's idiomatic nuances.

In the pursuit of a deeper understanding of the translation nuances concerning idioms in *The Scholars*, the author undertakes a meticulous quantitative analysis of the idiomatic expressions translated into English. This careful enumeration and examination of the idioms aim to shed light on the translation choices made and their implications for the conveyance of cultural and linguistic subtleties. By systematically calculating the frequency and nature of idiomatic translations, the author endeavors to uncover patterns that reveal the translators' strategies in bridging the cultural and linguistic divides between the original Chinese text and its English rendition.

This quantitative approach to analyzing idiom translation within *The Scholars* not only provides a foundation for assessing the extent of normalization versus deviation but also contributes to the broader discourse on translation theory and practice. Through this detailed investigation, the author aspires to enhance the understanding of how idioms, as carriers of deep cultural significance and linguistic richness, are navigated in the process of translation, offering insights into the complexity and challenges inherent in rendering culturally embedded expressions into another language.

Idiom Translation Features Presented in *The Scholars* are detailed in Table 5.9.

Table 5.9 Idiom Translation Features Presented in *The Scholars*

Category	Normalized Translation	Ratio of Normalized Translation	Deviated Translation	Ratio of Deviated Translation	Ellipsis	Ratio of Ellipsis	Total Number
two-part allegorical sayings	5	56%	2	22%	2	22%	9
colloquialisms	10	43.48%	13	56.52%	0	0	23
proverbs	9	36%	16	64%	0	0	25
set phrases	50	66%	23	30%	3	4%	76
in total	74	55.6%	54	40.6%	5	3.8%	133

Upon detailed analysis, it emerges that out of a total of 133 idioms analyzed in the translation of *The Scholars*, a significant portion, specifically 74 idioms, exhibited traits of normalization, representing approximately 55% of all idioms evaluated. This suggests a predominant inclination towards adapting these idiomatic expressions in a way that resonates more naturally with the linguistic and cultural framework of the target language. On the other hand, 54 idioms, or roughly 41%, demonstrated a deviation from the original expressions, opting to preserve the unique cultural and linguistic nuances inherent in the source text. The comparative analysis of these figures underscores a marked preference for normalization over deviation in the translation approach adopted for Chinese idioms within *The Scholars*. This trend indicates that the translators were more inclined to ensure that the idiomatic expressions were rendered in a manner that would be readily comprehensible and culturally appropriate for the English-speaking audience, thereby facilitating a smoother reading experience while still attempting to maintain the essence of the original text.

5.1.4 Sanitization and Contamination

Sanitization and contamination in translation practices pertain to the strategic decision to either eliminate or retain certain expressions that are deeply rooted in cultural taboos, ethical considerations, values, ideologies, and religious beliefs, particularly when these elements starkly contrast with or potentially offend the sensibilities of the target language's culture. This intricate process involves navigating through a linguistic landscape where slang, explicit sexual descriptions (including references to homosexuality, sexual perversion, incest, etc.), ideologies that clash with prevailing beliefs, pagan teachings juxtaposed with mainstream religious doctrines, and portrayals that cast the target culture in a negative light come into play. Hu Xianyao (2006) elucidates this concept, highlighting the delicate balance that translators must strike in order to respect the cultural thresholds of the target audience.

Regardless of a culture's degree of openness or tolerance, there are inherent limits to its acceptance of foreignness, especially when such elements are perceived as "polluting" or threatening to the integrity and values of the native language and culture. In these instances, the act of removing or "sanitizing" content deemed "dangerous" becomes not just a choice but a necessity to ensure the translated work is palatable and respectful to the target audience. This process of sanitization is not arbitrary but is instead carefully calibrated to align with the prevailing expectation norms of the period, reflecting a deep understanding of the target culture's boundaries and sensitivities.

In the context of *Ru Lin Wai Shi* and its English translation by the Yangs, this dynamic of sanitization and contamination is vividly illustrated through specific examples. These instances shed light on the translators' meticulous approach to rendering the text in a way that both honors the original's essence and navigates the potential cultural pitfalls that could alienate or offend the target readership. By selectively sanitizing the text, the Yangs demonstrate an acute awareness of the cultural and ideological landscape of their audience, making calculated decisions to either tone down or entirely omit elements that could disrupt the cultural harmony or coherence of the translation.

Furthermore, the act of contamination, wherein certain elements are retained despite their potential clash with the target culture's norms, speaks to a deliberate choice to challenge or expand the cultural horizons of the audience, inviting them to engage with the source culture's complexity and nuances on a deeper level. This careful balancing act between sanitization and contamination underscores the nuanced role of the translator as both a cultural mediator and an educator, tasked with bridging disparate worlds while respecting their distinct boundaries and identities.

Through the analysis of *Ru Lin Wai Shi*, we gain insight into the ethical and cultural considerations that underpin the translation process, highlighting the nuanced decisions that translators must make to ensure that their work resonates with the target audience while faithfully conveying the source text's intended messages and cultural depth.

㉜ ST: 邹吉甫道："阿弥陀佛！二位少老爷是肯做好事的。想着从前已往，不知拔济了多少人。"

TT: "Amida Buddha!" exclaimed Zou. "How eager you two gentlemen are to do good! Heaven only knows how many poor people you have helped in the past..."

㉝ ST: 顺姑娘道："阿弥陀佛！可见人要做好人，到这时候就见出分晓来了！"

TT: "Amida Buddha! It shows you've got to be good!" cried Miss Shun. "At a time like that men appear in their true colours!"

The phrase "阿弥陀佛," which translates to "Amida Buddha" in Sanskrit, holds profound significance within the Buddhist tradition, representing not just the name of a revered Buddha but also serving as a ubiquitous symbol of Buddhism itself. This expression transcends religious boundaries to become a familiar term across China, permeating various aspects of daily life and cultural practices. Regardless of an individual's religious affiliation, "阿弥陀佛" finds its way into the vernacular, employed in diverse contexts that extend beyond the confines of Buddhist ritual and doctrine.

In the rich tapestry of Chinese culture, invoking "阿弥陀佛" serves multiple purposes. It is not uncommon for people to utter "Amida Buddha" in response to hearing about grievous events or instances of grave injustice. This exclamation is not merely a reflex but a conscious invocation of Buddhist principles, symbolizing a denouncement of cruelty, a call for compassion, and an expression of solidarity and empathy towards those who suffer. Such usage reflects the deeply ingrained values of leniency and mercy that Buddhism espouses, demonstrating how religious expressions can evolve into broader cultural idioms that convey shared moral and ethical standards.

The adaptability of "阿弥陀佛" is further illustrated in its application to comment on the moral fabric of society. For instance, when used to commend altruistic acts, as seen in Example ㉜, the phrase echoes Buddhism's advocacy for kindness and generosity towards the less fortunate. This alignment with Buddhist teachings on compassion underscores the phrase's role in reinforcing social virtues and encouraging benevolent behavior. Similarly, in Example ㉝, where the expression is deployed to articulate the concept of karmic justice—reward for virtue and retribution for vice—it encapsulates a core tenet of Buddhism that resonates with universal notions of moral accountability and cosmic balance.

The translators' choice to render "阿弥陀佛" directly as "Amida Buddha" in the English version of the text is a strategic one, aimed at preserving the cultural and religious specificity of the original expression. By opting for a literal translation, the translators afford target readers a window into the spiritual landscape of China, where Buddhism holds a place of reverence akin to that of major deities in other religious traditions. This approach enables readers unfamiliar with Chinese culture to grasp the significance of "Buddha" within the context of reverence, devotion, and everyday discourse, bridging cultural and spiritual gaps through the narrative.

Furthermore, the unaltered translation allows English-speaking readers to appreciate the nuances of "阿弥陀佛"'s usage within Chinese society—how it transcends mere religious invocation to become a medium through which values of mercy, justice, and humaneness are articulated. By encountering "Amida Buddha" in its various contextual applications, readers gain insights into the interplay between language, religion, and culture in China, fostering a deeper understanding of how religious expressions can embody and propagate ethical principles and societal norms.

In essence, the translation of "阿弥陀佛" into "Amida Buddha" not only conveys the linguistic meaning of the term but also invites readers to explore the philosophical and cultural dimensions it encompasses. Through this nuanced translation choice, the target audience is offered a glimpse into the profound impact of Buddhism on Chinese thought, language, and social conduct, enriching their comprehension of the text and facilitating a more informed and empathetic engagement with Chinese religious and cultural traditions.

㉞ ST: 恭喜荀小相公，而今挣了这一顶头巾，不枉了荀老爹一生忠厚，做多少佛面上的事，广积阴功。

TT: Congratulations, Mr. Xun, on becoming a scholar! This is a reward for all the good deeds your worthy father did to the glory of Buddha.

In the philosophical and spiritual framework of Buddhism, the concepts of karma and reincarnation hold that the virtuous actions performed by individuals throughout their lives are meticulously documented and subsequently rewarded in the afterlife. These accumulated merits, referred to as "阴功" or "阴德" in Buddhist doctrine, posit that both the individuals who enacted these good deeds and their descendants will, in due time, reap the benefits of these altruistic acts. This belief system underpins the notion prevalent among ancient Chinese communities that one's prosperity and success can often be traced back to the benevolent deeds executed by their forebears, a sentiment vividly illustrated in Example ㉞ from the text. However, such concepts steeped in the intricacies of Buddhist belief may pose comprehension challenges or encounter resistance from English readers, whose cultural and religious paradigms may not readily align with these ideas. Consequently, translators might find themselves in a position where they must judiciously decide to omit or alter certain elements of the original cultural content to better suit the sensibilities of the target audience.

Religious terminology, categorized as one of the six principal types of taboo in English, presents translators with a triad of methodological choices: literal translation, sanitization, and ellipsis. Literal translation endeavors to convey the source text's information with clarity and fidelity, whereas sanitization employs euphemisms or less sensitive alternatives to address potentially controversial or taboo subjects within the target language context. Ellipsis, on the other hand, involves the deliberate omission of sensitive material from the source text, aimed at circumventing potential reader discomfort or adhering to specific cultural norms (Hu Kaibao, 2014:218).

An examination of *The Scholars* reveals the presence of 52 religiously themed words. Utilizing the previously constructed parallel corpora, this study focuses on a selection of key terms encompassing both Buddhist and Taoist elements, such as "阿弥陀佛" (a term denoting Amitabha Buddha), "菩萨" (referring to Bodhisattvas or enlightened beings), "观音" (the Bodhisattva of compassion and wisdom), "法眼" (a Buddhist concept describing the Bodhisattva's ability to perceive the true nature of reality), "文昌殿" (a site dedicated to Taoist deities of literature), "关帝庙" (a temple complex honoring Taoist gods), among others, which encapsulate a diverse range of religious beliefs and practices. By analyzing the translation strategies employed for these terms, the study aims to uncover the prevailing norms regarding the treatment of religious content, specifically identifying tendencies toward either sanitization or contamination.

This analysis is predicated on retrieving instances of these terms within the Chinese text and their corresponding English translations, followed by a quantitative assessment of the varied translation methods utilized. The goal is to discern the overarching patterns in how religious expressions are rendered in the translation, thereby shedding light on the translators' approaches to navigating the delicate balance between fidelity to the source material and sensitivity to the target culture's norms and values. The findings, summarized in Table 5.10, provide invaluable insights into the translational norms governing the inclusion or exclusion of religious content, offering a nuanced understanding of how cultural and spiritual elements are adapted for an audience potentially unfamiliar with the source text's religious and philosophical underpinnings.

Through this comprehensive exploration of religious term translation in *The Scholars*, the study not only illuminates the strategies adopted to bridge cultural and spiritual divides but also contributes to a broader dialogue on the role of translation in mediating between diverse worldviews, enhancing our appreciation of the complexity inherent in conveying religious and cultural nuance across linguistic barriers.

Table 5.10 The English Translation about Religious Words in *The Scholars*

Translation Methods	The Source Text	The Translation Version	Frequency	Total Frequency	Percentage
literal translation	菩萨	statue of a bodhisattva	1	23	44.23%
		bodhisattva	1		
		Buddha	7		
	阿弥陀佛	Amida Buddha	4		
	观音	Guanyin	9		
		Buddhist	1		
sanitization	菩萨	shrine	2	22	42.31%
		images	1		
		granny	3		
		God	2		
	阿弥陀佛	Gracious Heaven	1		
	观音	goddess	1		
	法眼	distinguished notice	1		
		most discriminating	1		
	文昌殿	temples to the God of Literature	1		
	关帝庙	temples to the God of War	1		
	阴功	good deeds	2		
	丹室	laboratory	2		
	内丹	yoga	1		
	外丹	chemistry	1		
	挂单	mendicant	1		
	法船	barges	1		

Cont.

Translation Methods	**The Source Text**	**The Translation Version**	**Frequency**	**Total Frequency**	**Percentage**
ellipsis	菩萨	省译	3	7	13.46%
	观音	省译	4		
in total			52	52	100%

Table 5.10 reveals that literal translations of religious terms in *The Scholars* account for 44.23% of the instances studied, while sanitization strategies—where sensitive terms are rendered through euphemisms or less controversial language—comprise 42.31%. Ellipsis, the practice of omitting certain religious content, constitutes 13.46% of the translation approaches employed. Thus, it is evident that although sanitization is a notable strategy, its prevalence is closely matched by literal translations, indicating that the tendency towards sanitization, while present, is not overwhelmingly dominant in the translation process.

5.1.5 Explicitness and Implicitness

"Explicitness" in translation refers to the tendency to elucidate and detail aspects in the translated text that might be left unsaid or implied in the original, effectively including additional background information to bridge cultural or contextual gaps between the source and target languages (Zanettin, 2014:16). Conversely, "implicitness" denotes a scenario where the meaning or information inherent in the source language remains unstated or subtly suggested within the specific context of the target language, relying on the reader's inferential reasoning to grasp the intended message

(Hu Kaibao, 2011).

To examine the dynamics of explicitness versus implicitness in *The Scholars*, this study embarks on an analysis beginning with the English translation of Chinese connectives and progressing to statistical evaluations of implicitness within the text. Connectives, as functional words, play a crucial role in bridging linguistic units, ranging from words and phrases to clauses, sentences, and even larger textual segments (Zhang Bin, Zhang Yi Sheng, 2000:140-195). Their utility extends beyond mere syntactic linkage, facilitating logical coherence and textual cohesion.

Chinese connectives are traditionally categorized based on their semantic roles into two primary types: coordinative conjunctions and modification-center conjunctions. Coordinative conjunctions further break down into subcategories such as coordinators, sequential connectives, progressive conjunctions, alternatives, and interpretative conjunctions. Modification-center conjunctions encompass causal, transitional, conditional, hypothetical, and objective relations (Huang Borong, Liao Xudong, 2014:128-133). Given the extensive array of conjunctions in Chinese, this study narrows its focus to those indicating transition, causality, condition, and coordination within the Chinese-English parallel corpus of *The Scholars*, utilizing PowerGREP 4 software for corpus retrieval. Target conjunctions include "但(但是)""却""因(因为，因此，因而)""既(既然)""只要""除非""才""又", and "而", with the aim of quantifying the corresponding and implicit instances to ascertain the degree of explicitness or implicitness manifested in the translation.

The methodology involves employing PowerGREP 4 to identify instances of selected logical conjunctions within *The Scholars* corpus, followed by an assessment of their frequency and the derivation of implicit examples. This process entails calculating the frequency of direct translations for conjunctions such as " 却 " and deducting this from the total number of sentences to determine the count of sentences where the conjunctions are implied rather than explicitly stated.

Subsequent statistical analysis of these logical relations aids in discerning the variance in data representation, shedding light on the translational strategies employed. This step is pivotal in understanding the nuances of explicitness or implicitness that pervade the English rendition of *The Scholars*. The comparative study of conjunction usage between the original Chinese text and its English translation reveals insightful patterns and tendencies, which are meticulously documented in Table 5.11.

This analytical approach, grounded in the disparities between English and Chinese linguistic structures and conventions, unveils the translational choices that underscore either an explicit or implicit conveyance of information in *The Scholars*. By dissecting the translation of conjunctions and evaluating their application within the narrative, this investigation enriches our comprehension of how explicitness and implicitness are navigated in the process of adapting a richly contextual Chinese classic for an English-speaking audience. Through this lens, the study contributes to a deeper understanding of cross-linguistic and cross-cultural translation practices, highlighting the intricacies and challenges inherent in faithfully rendering the subtleties of the source language while ensuring accessibility and coherence in the target language.

Table 5.11 The English Translation of the Conjunctions in *The Scholars*

LOGICAL RELATION-SHIP	CONJUNC-TION	TOTAL SENTENCES	CORRESPON-DENCES	IMPLICI-TNESS	RATIO OF IMPLICITNESS (%)
transition	但（但是）	85	73	12	14
	却	241	137	104	43
cause and effect	因（因为、因此、因而）	253	145	108	43
	既（既然）	73	63	10	14
condition	只要	25	16	9	36
	除非	5	5	0	0
	才	159	95	64	40
coordinators	又	1,022	746	276	27
	而	195	132	63	32

The examination of logical relationships within *The Scholars* through both implicit and explicit instances is detailed in the outcomes presented in Table 5.12.

Table 5.12 The Comparison between Logical Relationships in *The Scholars*

LOGICAL RELATION-SHIP	TOTAL SENTENCES	CORRESPON-DENCES	RATIO OF CORRESPON-DENCES(%)	IMPLICIT-NESS	RATIO OF IMPLICIT-NESS(%)
transition	326	210	65%	116	35%
cause and effect	326	208	64%	118	36%

Cont.

LOGICAL RELATION-SHIP	TOTAL SENTENCES	CORRESPON-DENCES	RATIO OF CORRESPON-DENCES(%)	IMPLICIT-NESS	RATIO OF IMPLICIT-NESS(%)
condition	189	116	61%	73	39%
coordinators	1217	878	72%	339	28%
in total	2,058	1,412	69%	646	31%

The comprehensive analysis of logical relationships within *The Scholars* as depicted in Table 5.12 reveals a predominantly explicit translation strategy, with a significant portion (69%) of connectives translated in a manner that corresponds directly to their usage in the source text. This leaves a smaller fraction (31%) where the connectives are implied rather than explicitly translated, indicating a preference for making the logical connections within the text clear to the reader.

The distribution of connective types further highlights the translators' approach, with coordinative relations being most frequently translated, followed by transitional, causal, and finally conditional connectives. This hierarchy not only reflects the complexity and nuance of the source text's logical structure but also underscores the translators' focus on maintaining narrative coherence and logical clarity in the English rendition.

The translation strategies employed for these connectives are multifaceted:

Diversity in Connective Use: The English translation utilizes a wide array of connectives to accurately mirror the logical relationships present in the original text.

(1) Coordinative relations are rendered with precision, ensuring that the additive, adversative, causal, and temporal relationships between clauses and sentences are preserved.

㉟ ST: 这人姓翟，是诸暨县一个头役，又是买办。因秦老的儿子秦大汉拜在他名下，叫他干爷，所以常时下乡来看亲家。

TT: This newcomer's name was Zhai. He was a county runner and also a bailiff, but since Old Qin's son was his godchild he often came to the village to visit their family.

(2) Transitional connectives guide the reader through the narrative, marking shifts in time, place, or topic with clarity.

㊱ ST: 时知县此时心中十分恼怒，本要立即差人拿了王冕来责惩一番，又想恐怕危老师说他暴躁，且忍口气回去，慢慢向老师说明此人不中抬举，再处置他也不迟。

TT: Thoroughly annoyed, his first impulse was to tell his attendants to arrest Wang Mian and punish him. Afraid, however, that Mr. Wei would call him hotheaded, he decided to swallow his anger and go back to explain to his patron that Wang Mian did not deserve to be honoured. He could punish the fellow later.

(3) A hypothetical relation in linguistics and translation refers to a logical connection between two or more clauses where one clause expresses a condition that is necessary for the realization of the situation described in the other clause.

㊲ ST: 古人说得好，<Y>‘作文之心如人目’，凡人目中，尘土屑固不可有，即金玉屑又是着得的么？

TT: How right the ancients were when they said: 'In writing an essay the mind should remain as clear as the human eye. It must hold no dust, not even of jade or gold.

In the three examples mentioned, the translators employ "and also," "however," and "not even" to make the logical connections of " 又 " more explicit.

Dual Connective Application: In cases where the source text employs a single conjunction, the translation introduces an additional connective to elucidate the underlying logical connection. This approach is particularly evident in complex sentences where a single connective in the source text might be insufficient to convey the nuanced relationships between clauses in English. By employing dual connectives, the translation disambiguates these relationships, enhancing the text's coherence and the reader's understanding.

㊳ ST: 新买了住宅，比京里钟楼街的房子还大些，值得二千两银子。因老先生要买，房主人让了几十两银卖了，图个名望体面。

TT: His new house is even bigger than the one in Bell Tower Street in the capital. The price was two thousand taels of silver, but, because the purchaser was so distinguished, the owner allowed him several dozen taels discount for the sake of the credit he would get from this transaction.

㊴ ST: 他会念诗，常拿些诗来求讲，公孙也略替他讲讲。因心里喜他殷勤，就把收的王观察的个旧枕箱把与他盛花儿针线，又无意中把遇见王观察这一件事向他说了。

TT: Shuang-hong could read poems and often brought verses for him to explain to her; and because Qu liked her, he gave her as a work-box the old casket presented to him by Prefect Wang, and inadvertently told her how he had met this rebel.

㊵ ST: 每收租时候，亲自到乡里佃户家，佃户备两样菜与老伯吃，老人家退去一样才吃一样。

TT: When the time came for collecting rent, he would go down to the country to visit the tenants himself; and if they prepared two dishes for him, he would send one away and eat one only.

In the given examples, the translation technique showcases the adaptability in handling the causal connective "因" from the source text. In the first two instances, the translators have skillfully rendered "因" into English by using a combination of causal and conjunctive elements. Specifically, they have employed "because" to establish causality, complemented by "and" to denote conjunction, and "but" to introduce a contrastive element, thereby enriching the textual coherence and logical flow in the target language. In the third example, the conditional aspect signaled by "only" in the source text is effectively translated as "and+if", a construction that neatly encapsulates the conditional relationship. This nuanced approach not only preserves the original meaning but also adapts it to the syntactic and stylistic conventions of English, demonstrating the translators' adeptness at navigating between languages to maintain clarity and fidelity to the source content.

Repositioning Relational Words: Another noteworthy strategy is the repositioning of relational words within the sentence structure. This adjustment is undertaken to align the translated sentences more closely with English syntactic norms, thereby making the logical relations between textual elements more explicit. Such repositioning is a testament to the translators' meticulous attention to detail and their commitment to preserving the logical integrity of the original while adapting it to the target language's grammatical framework.

㊶ ST: 只有隔壁秦老，虽然务农，却是个有意思的人。因自小看见他长大，如此不俗，所以敬他爱他，时时和他亲热，邀在草堂里坐着说话儿。

TT: Only his neighbour, Old Qin, realized how remarkable he was; for Old Qin was an intelligent man, though a peasant, and he had seen Wang Mian grow up. He respected and loved Wang Mian, and often asked him to his thatched cottage to talk with him.

In the provided example, the arrangement of the causal connective is altered in the translation, making the logical relationship within the translated sentences more clearly defined.

The detailed examination reveals that the utilization of connectives within the source text predominantly adheres to a strategy of direct translation, effectively unveiling the underlying logical relationships that might otherwise remain obscure. This strategic choice ensures that the translation delivers a clearer and more comprehensible grammatical interplay among the constituent words, phrases, and sentences, significantly enhancing the explicitness of the translated text. Such explicitness not only clarifies the intended message but also simplifies the semantic complexity inherent in the original Chinese text, which is characterized by its use of parataxis—a structural feature that tends to present ideas in a sequence without clear connective markers, thereby introducing a level of ambiguity.

By adopting an explicit translation approach, the translators effectively mitigate this ambiguity, rendering the translated content more accessible to the target audience. This process of semantic simplification, facilitated by the explicitness operation norm, underscores the translators' commitment to producing a text that resonates with the linguistic and cognitive frameworks of the target language speakers. Consequently, the explicitness inherent in the translation process not only serves to illuminate the original text's meaning more clearly but also aligns the translation with the expectations and conventions of the target language culture, thereby enhancing its readability and overall acceptability. Through this meticulous approach to translating connectives and clarifying logical relationships, the translation achieves a balance between fidelity to the source text and adaptation to the target language's norms, exemplifying the nuanced art of translation.

In sum, the explicitness observed in the translation of *The Scholars* serves multiple functions: it clarifies the logical structure of the narrative, simplifies complex semantic relationships for the target audience, and reduces ambiguity inherent in the paratactic nature of the Chinese language. This explicitness, as a manifestation of the operational norm, not only enhances the readability of the translation but also plays a crucial role in bridging the cultural and linguistic gap between the source and target texts. Through careful application of diverse connectives, dual conjunctions, and thoughtful repositioning of relational words, the translation achieves a delicate balance between fidelity to the source material and adaptability to the target language, thereby facilitating a deeper understanding and appreciation of *The Scholars* among English-speaking readers.

5.2 The Reasons for the Adoption of the Translation Norms in *The Scholars*

Translation norms represent the collective values and expectations of a community, deeply rooted in the social and cultural fabric of the time. These norms exert a profound influence on the translator's mindset, guiding their choices and infusing their work with both the spirit of the era and a unique personal flair. In examining the translation norms applied to *The Scholars*, it becomes imperative to contextualize these norms within the specific cultural backdrop in which the translation efforts took place. This entails a thorough exploration of the socio-cultural dynamics that contributed to shaping these norms, offering insights into how they came to be and their impact on the translation process. By delving into this complex interplay of societal values, historical context, and individual creativity, we can gain a deeper understanding of the forces that mold translation practices and the nuanced ways in which translators navigate these influences to produce work that resonates with both their personal style and the expectations of their time.

5.2.1 The background of the Social Culture

Since the onset of the 20th century, Chinese culture has faced challenges of transition and adaptation. As Wu Guangjun (2014:164) astutely observes, classical Chinese was becoming increasingly rigid, while the vernacular, though emerging, lacked the robustness to fully assert itself. This period of linguistic and cultural flux in China contrasted sharply with the situation in the United States during the 1950s, a time marked by considerable social stability and cultural prosperity.

The 1950s in the United States were characterized by a sense of security and affluence. Under President Eisenhower's administration, the nation enjoyed peace, economic growth, and low unemployment. The suburban lifestyle flourished as a symbol of the American dream, bolstered by the country's dominant position on the global stage, both militarily and culturally. This era also witnessed a vibrant literary scene, enriched by a wide array of genres and voices, reflecting the nation's confidence and creative vitality.

In this context, the English language, with its "higher prestige," was less receptive to the influences of translated works from languages such as Chinese, which were perceived as coming from a culturally and linguistically "declining" tradition. This led to a translation practice that favored convention over innovation, aiming to adhere closely to the norms and stylistic preferences of the target language and culture. Translators, thus, were more inclined to minimize the "interference" of the source text's linguistic and cultural peculiarities, opting instead for strategies that would ensure the translated text's acceptability and intelligibility to English-speaking audiences.

The preference for convention in translation can also be attributed to the inherent characteristics of the English language system itself. Translation, as an act of linguistic and cultural exchange, not only transfers content but also interacts with and potentially alters the linguistic expression forms of the target language. However, such alterations are constrained by the existing grammatical resources and norms of the target language. The degree to which a translated text can be integrated into the target language's grammatical system without being marginalized or deemed "foreign" is largely determined by the target language's own dynamics and state of development.

In the stable linguistic ecosystem of mid-20th century American English, the system was less open to the disruptive influences of translated texts, especially those from languages with significantly different grammatical structures and cultural references. This stability meant that translations from Chinese to English during this period were more likely to conform to established norms and patterns of the target language, emphasizing clarity, coherence, and cultural familiarity over the preservation of the source text's unique stylistic or conceptual elements.

The translation of *Ru Lin Wai Shi* into English exemplifies this trend. In its English rendition, the text exhibits a marked preference for convention, both in the choice of lexical items and in the construction of textual coherence. This approach results in a translation that, while perhaps sacrificing some of the source text's original flavor and cultural specificity, achieves a form and style that align with the expectations and preferences of English-speaking readers.

Such a translation strategy, while pragmatic, underscores the complex interplay between linguistic fidelity, cultural authenticity, and readability in translation practice. It reflects a careful balancing act performed by translators, who must navigate the dual imperatives of honoring the source text's integrity and ensuring the translated work's acceptance within the target cultural and linguistic context. This balancing act is shaped not only by the translators' skill and sensibility but also by the broader sociolinguistic and cultural dynamics that define the relationship between the source and target languages at any given moment in history.

In summary, the translation of *The Scholars* into English during a period of American cultural ascendancy and linguistic stability reveals much about the priorities and pressures that shape translation decisions. It highlights the extent to which translations are products of their time, reflecting the cultural attitudes, linguistic norms, and social conditions that prevail in the target language environment. As such, translations serve as fascinating lenses through which to view the intercultural exchanges and shifts in global cultural dynamics that characterize our interconnected world.

5.2.2 The Translator's Factor

Following the establishment of the People's Republic of China and leading into the era of reform and opening up, the nation's approach to foreign culture and translation policy was characterized by strategic clarity. This period marked a crucial phase in China's cultural diplomacy, with translation serving as a key instrument for international cultural exchange. In this context, the translation endeavors of Yang Hsien-yi and Gladys Yang stand out for their adherence to realism and a commitment to presenting foreign literature in a manner that remained faithful to the source texts.

Yang Hsien-yi's philosophy towards translation was deeply influenced by his understanding of the translator's duty to the source material. Rejecting the notion that translations should be laden with explanatory notes, Yang advocated for a form of fidelity that transcended mere literalness. His approach was grounded in the belief that the essence of translation lay in the accurate conveyance of meaning from one language to another, rather than in a slavish adherence to the source text's form. This perspective on translation fidelity, focusing on semantic rather than syntactic loyalty, reflects a nuanced understanding of the interlingual transfer process.

Gladys Yang, co-translator and spouse of Yang Hsien-yi, brought a complementary set of skills and sensibilities to their joint translation projects. Her role often involved refining and enhancing the initial drafts to ensure that the translations not only captured the meaning of the original works but also resonated with target language readers. Gladys's unique position, straddling both Chinese and Western cultural perspectives, allowed her to make linguistic and stylistic adjustments that aligned with the expectations of a diverse readership. This ability to navigate between cultures underscored the pragmatic aspect of their translation work, highlighting the importance of accessibility and reader engagement in the translation process.

The translation of *The Scholars*, a seminal work in Chinese literature, exemplifies the Yangs' translation philosophy. An analysis of the parallel corpus reveals strategic omissions and adaptations that serve to streamline the text, making it more accessible to readers unfamiliar with the dense and allusive style characteristic of classical Chinese literature. Phrases like "光天化日" (broad daylight) and "忍气吞声" (to swallow one's anger) are rendered in a manner that emphasizes clarity and conciseness, reflecting a deliberate effort to simplify the language without diluting the original meaning.

This approach to translation is indicative of the Yangs' deep understanding of their audience's needs and the broader social function of translation. By tailoring their translations to enhance readability and cultural relatability, the Yangs demonstrated an acute awareness of the social dimension of translation. Their work is a testament to the belief that translations should bridge cultural divides, facilitating a dialogue between the source text's culture and the target audience's cultural context.

Moreover, the Yangs' translations during this period reflect the broader cultural and political milieu in which they operated. Their work was conducted under the auspices of a national translation policy that sought to introduce foreign literary works to Chinese audiences in a way that was both respectful of the original texts and cognizant of the ideological and aesthetic sensibilities of the time. This balancing act between fidelity to the source material and the exigencies of the target culture highlights the complex interplay between translation, cultural policy, and cross-cultural communication.

In sum, the translation practices of Yang Hsien-yi and Gladys Yang during the transformative years of New China's formation and subsequent opening to the world exemplify a model of translation that is both deeply respectful of the source material and attentively attuned to the target audience's expectations. Their work serves as a valuable case study in the art and science of translation, offering insights into the ways in which translations can serve as conduits for cultural exchange, understanding, and dialogue. Through their meticulous approach to translation, the Yangs not only made significant contributions to the global appreciation of Chinese literature but also laid the groundwork for future generations of translators navigating the complexity of intercultural communication.

5.2.3 Poetics

In the intricate process of translating literary works, the interaction between operation norms, particularly the interplay of convention and foreignness, is far from being dichotomous. Rather, it embodies a dynamic and nuanced relationship, akin to the concept of "rhythm" in poetics as discussed by Henri Meschonnic. This notion of rhythm encompasses the entirety of experiences that impact speakers, suggesting that every linguistic event is not merely a recapitulation of what preceded but an emergence of something uniquely novel and distinct. This theoretical framework offers a profound insight into understanding the fluid nature of translation norms within literary translation, particularly in the context of *The Scholars*.

The examination of the translation of *Ru Lin Wai Shi* reveals a tapestry woven with threads of both conventional norms and elements of foreignness. Instances such as the translation of phrases like "风餐露宿" (braving the wind and dew), "如雷灌耳" (resounds like thunder), and "白刀子进去，红刀子出来" (every day the blade goes in white and comes out red) exemplify this interweaving. These examples illuminate the translators' adeptness in navigating between staying true to the source text's cultural nuances and making the text accessible and resonant for the target audience. It is this delicate balance that encapsulates the essence of translation as an art form—straddling the line between similarity and dissimilarity, between the familiar and the foreign.

The relationship between convention and foreignness in translation can be likened to a dialogue between similarity and dissimilarity, where each bears traces of the other. "Dissimilarity" emerges from the realm of "similarity," implying that true "similarity" must, inherently, accommodate "dissimilarity." This evolving "similarity" is continually renewed, reflecting the dynamic and reciprocal nature of cultural exchange through translation. It is only through altering the "rhythm" of the target language that the distinctiveness of the "foreign" can be truly appreciated. Simultaneously, this acceptance of "foreignness" paves the way for the genesis of new linguistic and cultural paradigms.

This ongoing dialogue between the source and target cultures, mediated through the act of translation, allows for a continuous enrichment of the target language and culture. Each translation act brings with it the potential for innovation within the target linguistic and cultural milieu, challenging and expanding its boundaries. The process of translating *Ru Lin Wai Shi* serves as a microcosm of this broader phenomenon, where the infusion of foreign elements into the target language does not merely introduce new lexical or syntactic forms but invites a reevaluation and expansion of existing cultural narratives.

Moreover, the presence of foreignness within the conventional framework of the target language underscores the transformative potential of translation. It demonstrates how translation can act as a catalyst for cultural evolution, enabling the target culture to assimilate and reinterpret foreign concepts in a manner that resonates with its own unique cultural and linguistic identity. This transformative process is not unidirectional; rather, it is characterized by a mutual exchange that enriches both the source and target cultures, fostering a deeper understanding and appreciation of the complexity of human expression across linguistic and cultural divides.

In conclusion, the translation of *Ru Lin Wai Shi* exemplifies the intricate dance between adherence to conventional norms and the embrace of foreignness, a dynamic interplay that defines the essence of literary translation. Through this process, translation emerges not merely as a means of conveying meaning across linguistic barriers but as a profound act of cultural negotiation and creation. It is a testament to the power of translation to bridge worlds, to bring into being a shared space where the rhythm of language and culture is continually reimagined and reborn.

Chapter Six

Conclusion

This chapter serves as the culmination of the study, offering a comprehensive overview of the principal discoveries and insights garnered from the research. It meticulously outlines the implications these findings have for future inquiries in the field, suggesting avenues for deeper exploration and investigation. Additionally, this section provides a critical evaluation of the study's constraints, acknowledging areas where limitations may have impacted the results or interpretation. The chapter concludes by succinctly recapping the major points addressed in previous sections, ensuring a cohesive and coherent wrap-up of the research narrative, thereby facilitating a clear understanding of the study's scope, outcomes, and potential impact on future scholarly endeavors.

6.1 Major Findings

This research embarked on a detailed exploration of the translation norms within *The Scholars*, aiming to not only identify these norms but also to delve into the factors influencing their formation. To achieve these goals, the study employed a self-constructed corpus, leveraging it as a primary tool for data collection and analysis. This approach enabled a multifaceted examination of the translation process, focusing on four key areas: the type/token ratio, the distribution of parts of speech, translation methods, and a comparative analysis of conjunctions concerning their implicitness and explicitness.

One of the initial observations was that the English rendition of *Ru Lin Wai Shi* adheres to certain operation norms that significantly influence the translation's overall character. Firstly, a noticeable simplification was observed in the lexical variability and the average sentence length, suggesting a deliberate effort to make the text more accessible to the target audience. Secondly, the translation exhibits a closer alignment with the typical characteristics of original English texts in terms of part-of-speech distribution. This alignment includes a tendency towards simplification, hypotaxis, and explicitness, which are achieved through various linguistic techniques such as the transformation of parts of speech, substitution, and ellipsis. Moreover, the analysis revealed that while the translation generally favors normalization in the rendition of idioms, deviations from this norm are evident in the translation of colloquialisms and proverbs, indicating a nuanced approach to preserving the source text's cultural and stylistic elements.

Another significant finding was the predominance of literal translations in the treatment of religious terminology. This choice suggests an intention to maintain the original text's cultural and religious nuances, thereby providing the target readership with a window into the source culture's spiritual and ideological landscape. Furthermore, the study noted a pronounced explicitness in the translation of connectives, pointing to a deliberate effort to enhance clarity and coherence in the translated text.

The research also highlighted the coexistence of convention and foreignness expectation norms within the English version of *Ru Lin Wai Shi*, with the former playing a dominant role and the latter taking on a subsidiary position. This dynamic suggests a complex interplay between the desire to make the text accessible and familiar to the target audience and the intent to preserve its foreignness and originality to some extent.

In delving into the factors that shape these translation norms, the study considered various dimensions, including the socio-cultural background, the translators' individual perspectives and methodologies, and the overarching poetics influencing the translation process. The socio-cultural context, particularly the historical and literary milieu in which the translation was undertaken, emerged as a critical determinant of the translation norms. This context includes the translators' personal experience, their philosophical and aesthetic orientations, and their interactions with both the source and target cultures.

The translators themselves, with their unique blend of linguistic proficiency, cultural insight, and creative intuition, play a pivotal role in the formation of translation norms. Their choices reflect a complex amalgamation of fidelity to the source text, responsiveness to the target audience's expectations, and adherence to the aesthetic and ethical standards of the target language and culture.

Finally, the concept of poetics, as it relates to translation, provides a valuable lens through which to understand the subtleties of the translation process. The study's analysis of poetics underscores the significance of rhythm, style, and narrative structure in shaping the translated text's reception and impact, further illuminating the intricate balance between convention and foreignness in translation norms.

In summary, this comprehensive investigation into the translation norms of *The Scholars* sheds light on the multifaceted nature of translation as a cultural and linguistic endeavor. It underscores the importance of considering a wide range of factors, from linguistic strategies and stylistic preferences to socio-cultural influences and individual translator choices, in understanding and evaluating the complexity of translation practice.

This study offers a comprehensive and systematic examination of the linguistic characteristics present in the English translation of *Ru Lin Wai Shi*, known as *The Scholars*. This in-depth analysis focuses on two primary aspects: word usage and syntactic structure, shedding light on the intricate processes and decisions underlying the translation.

In terms of word usage, several key trends are evident in *The Scholars* when compared to its original Chinese text. Firstly, there is a noticeable simplification in the use of vocabulary. This simplification is not merely about reducing the complexity of words but also involves selecting terms that are more familiar and accessible to the target audience, thus enhancing the readability and comprehensibility of the translation. Secondly, the translation exhibits a significant reduction in the frequency of nouns, particularly proper names. This reduction may be attributed to a conscious effort to streamline the text and make it more relatable to readers unfamiliar with the cultural and historical context of the original. Thirdly, there is an increase in the usage of pronouns in the English version. This rise in pronoun frequency serves to maintain narrative coherence and fluidity, compensating for the reduced use of specific nouns and names.

The syntactic structure of *The Scholars* further underscores the translation's linguistic adaptations. The average sentence length in the English version is notably shorter than that typically observed in texts written by educated English speakers. This brevity can be attributed to a strategic effort to simplify the text's structure, making it more digestible for readers. Additionally, the translation displays a pronounced tendency towards hypotaxis, characterized by a significant increase in the use of prepositions and conjunctions. This shift towards a more hypotactic structure enhances the clarity and logic of the translation, facilitating a smoother reading experience.

Moreover, the frequent employment of explicit conjunctions over their implicit counterparts in the English version underscores a deliberate choice to make logical relationships and transitions within the text more overt. By clearly articulating the connections between ideas and sections, the translation ensures that readers can easily follow the narrative flow and understand the underlying logic of the original work.

The explicitness in conjunction use and the preference for a hypotactic syntactic structure reflect a broader trend towards adapting the translation to meet the expectations and preference of the target audience. These linguistic features serve to bridge cultural and linguistic gaps, making the rich narrative and complex characters of *The Scholars* accessible to a wider audience. By carefully selecting words and structuring sentences, the translators have crafted a version of the text that honors the original's essence while also appealing to readers' linguistic sensibilities.

This meticulous attention to linguistic detail in *The Scholars* not only highlights the translators' skill and sensitivity but also contributes to the ongoing dialogue about translation strategies and their impact on cross-cultural literary exchange. The study's findings provide valuable insights into the balance between maintaining the source text's integrity and ensuring the translation's accessibility and enjoyment for the target audience. Through this analysis, the study underscores the complexity of translation as an art form, one that requires a deep understanding of both the source and target languages, as well as a nuanced appreciation of the cultural contexts that shape them.

6.2 Implications

The investigation into the English rendition of *Ru Lin Wai Shi* has yielded insights affirming adherence to established translation norms, illuminating the nuanced interplay between convention and foreignness expectations in the translators' lexical selections. This study has not only identified the prevailing norms guiding translation practices but has also begun to unravel the complex web of factors influencing these norms, including the social-cultural backdrop, poetic elements, and the translators' personal experience. The identification of these norms and their impact on word choice is pivotal, offering a lens through which to understand the existence of the translation version and the intricacies of its linguistic fabric.

Despite these advances, the study has only scratched the surface in dissecting the full spectrum of influences shaping translation norms. The extent to which the broader social-cultural context, the specificities of literary poetics, and the individual experience of the translators have steered the adoption of certain norms, remains partially explored. These areas represent a fertile ground for further inquiry, suggesting a need for more comprehensive research to decode the multifaceted dynamics at play.

Further exploration into the social-cultural context could delve into how the translation of *Ru Lin Wai Shi* reflects or diverges from the prevailing values, beliefs, and literary trends of the time. This would involve a closer examination of the period's socio-political climate, literary movements, and public sentiments, seeking to understand how these external factors might have influenced the translators' decisions and the overall direction of the translation.

Additionally, a deeper analysis of poetics could illuminate how the aesthetic and stylistic choices made in the translation align with or challenge the poetic conventions of both the source and target languages. This line of inquiry would benefit from a comparative study of literary techniques, narrative structures, and thematic elements, aiming to uncover how the translators navigated the delicate balance between fidelity to the original text and the creative demands of translation as an art form.

The personal experience and backgrounds of the translators themselves also warrant closer scrutiny. Exploring their linguistic competencies, cultural exposures, and philosophical inclinations could offer valuable insights into how their identities and life stories have left an indelible mark on the translation. Such an investigation would contribute to a more nuanced understanding of the translation as a deeply personal, yet universally accessible, cultural artifact.

In light of these considerations, several research avenues present themselves. One potential direction is a cross-cultural study comparing translations of *Ru Lin Wai Shi* into different languages, which could shed light on the universal and culture-specific aspects of translation norms. Another avenue could involve longitudinal studies tracking the evolution of translation norms over time, offering a historical perspective on how changes in society and literature have influenced translation practices.

Moreover, empirical research employing qualitative and quantitative methodologies could further dissect the translators' choices, providing a richer, data-driven understanding of the translation process. Interviews, surveys, and textual analysis could complement the findings of this study, enriching the discourse on translation norms with diverse perspectives and empirical evidence.

In sum, the exploration of translation norms in *Ru Lin Wai Shi* opens up a vast field of inquiry, inviting further research to deepen our comprehension of the complex interrelations between text, culture, and individual agency in the translation process. The pursuit of these questions promises to enhance our appreciation of translation not just as a linguistic exercise but as a cultural endeavor that bridges worlds, enriches languages, and facilitates the global exchange of ideas.

Embarking on a journey through different historical epochs to scrutinize translation norms provides a fertile ground for uncovering the evolution and dynamic interplay of these norms across time. The intriguing prospect of applying a similar research design to translations from diverse historical periods beckons a comprehensive inquiry into how translation norms have been shaped by the cultural, social, and political milieus of their times. The fundamental question arises: Would the findings of this study align with those derived from translations belonging to varied historical contexts? Undertaking such diachronic research would not only enrich our understanding of translation norms but also illuminate the transformations these norms have undergone in response to changing societal values and literary trends.

Exploring translations across a broad temporal spectrum offers the unique advantage of capturing the nuances of behavioral change influenced by shifting translation norms. Such changes, often subtle and gradual, may remain obscured within the confines of a single version or a specific period. A diachronic approach, therefore, provides a panoramic view of the evolving landscape of translation practices, revealing patterns of adaptation, resistance, and innovation that have characterized the translation field over centuries.

Moreover, this longitudinal perspective allows for the examination of how external factors—such as technological advancements, global conflicts, and the rise and fall of literary movements—have exerted pressure on translation norms, prompting translators to adopt new strategies, techniques, and linguistic choices. By tracing these developments, researchers can gain insights into the forces driving the evolution of translation norms and how these norms, in turn, shape the translator's approach to the source text.

Further extending this research to encompass a wider array of texts and versions from different time periods would offer a richer dataset, enhancing the potential for deep insights into the effects of translation norms on linguistic and stylistic choices. Such an expansive study would not only chronicle the historical trajectory of translation norms but also shed light on the cyclical nature of certain trends and the emergence of new paradigms in response to evolving societal demands and expectations.

In addition to historical analysis, there is a pressing need for research that incorporates diverse perspectives and methodologies to assess translation norms more comprehensively. Incorporating ratings from a broad spectrum of reviewers, including translators, literary critics, linguists, and the target audience, would provide a multifaceted evaluation of translation norms. This approach would enable a more nuanced understanding of the consensus and divergence in perceptions of fidelity, creativity, and cultural sensitivity in translation practices.

Moreover, the selection of texts for analysis should be broadened to include a variety of genres, cultural contexts, and languages. By examining how translation norms manifest in different textual and cultural environments, researchers can uncover the universality and specificity of these norms, offering insights into the complex interplay between global translation trends and local cultural imperatives.

In conclusion, extending research into the diachronic study of translation norms and incorporating a wider array of perspectives and texts promises to unlock a treasure trove of knowledge about the evolution of translation practices. Such research could not only chronicle the historical development of translation norms but also anticipate future trends, offering valuable guidance for translators, scholars, and policymakers in navigating the ever-shifting terrain of global literature and cultural exchange.

6.3 Limitations

While this study has embarked on a comprehensive exploration of translation norms, delving deep into theoretical frameworks, meticulously detailing the linguistic characteristics of translated texts, and presenting an objective analysis of various translation norms, its scope and depth are inevitably circumscribed by several limitations. These constraints stem from the author's research capabilities, cognitive reach, and proficiency in utilizing corpus technologies and methodologies. Consequently, despite the rigorous effort to ensure a thorough investigation, several areas of potential weakness within the study must be acknowledged.

First and foremost, the temporal and resource constraints faced during the research process have led to limitations in the development of the *Ru Lin Wai Shi* corpus. The capacity of the corpus, its construction, and the extent to which it can truly represent *The Scholars* in its entirety are questions that merit further scrutiny. The representativeness of the corpus is a critical factor in the validity of the research findings, as it determines the extent to which conclusions drawn from the corpus can be generalized to the broader work. As such, the constrained capacity of the corpus may limit the comprehensiveness of the analysis and the applicability of the findings.

Moreover, the research findings are constrained by the inherent limitations of the tools and methods employed in the study. The reliance on limited corpus processing tools, such as Tokenizer and POS Tagger, coupled with the author's independent exploration in corpus construction, introduces potential inaccuracies in part-of-speech tagging and statistical analysis. These technical limitations could affect the precision of language feature statistics and analyses, particularly when investigating subtle linguistic elements. The accuracy and reliability of the corpus analysis are thus contingent on the effectiveness of the tools and methods utilized, underscoring the need for ongoing refinement and validation of corpus construction and analysis techniques.

Additionally, the study's reliance on a parallel corpus necessitated frequent references to theories of Chinese linguistics, grammar, and discourse. However, the author's lack of systematic training in Chinese linguistics may lead to a somewhat superficial discussion of these aspects. The complexity and nuance of Chinese linguistic structures and their implications for translation require a deep and nuanced understanding that can only be achieved through rigorous academic training and extensive research experience. As such, the exploration of Chinese linguistic features within the context of translation norms may not fully capture the intricacies and subtleties of the source language.

In conclusion, while this study represents a significant effort to explore translation norms and their manifestations in translated texts, it is important to recognize the limitations inherent in the research process. The capacity of the corpus, the tools and methods employed, and the depth of linguistic analysis are all factors that constrain the study's scope and depth. Acknowledging these limitations is crucial for contextualizing the findings and for guiding future research efforts. Further investigation, employing a more expansive corpus, advanced analytical tools, and a deeper engagement with linguistic theories, will be essential for building upon the foundations laid by this study and for advancing our understanding of translation norms and their impact on the practice of translation.

Notes

[1] This is a freeware program designed and developed by MINISTRY OF EDUCATION INSTITUTE OF APPLIED LINGUISTICS.

[2] This is a freeware program designed and developed by BFSU (Beijing Foreign Studies University)Corpus Research Group .

[3] They are chapter 1,2,3,5,6,7,9,10,11,13,14,15,17,18,19,21,22,23,25,26,27,29,30,31,33,34, 35,37,38,39,41,42,43,45,46,47,49,50,51,53,54 and 55.

[4] This is an online alignment tool which can be freely available at https://www.tmxmall.com.

[5] According to the "International English Usage", English taboos are divided into 6 categories, namely: religious, sexual, excretion, disease and death, social class and the age and weight (quoted from Hu Kaibao,2014:217).

References

CHESTERMAN A, 2012. *Memes of Translation: The Spread of Ideas in Translation Theory* [M]. Shanghai: Shanghai Foreign Language Education Press.

ZANETTIN F, 2014.*Translation-Driven Corpora* [M]. London and New York: Routledge.

HERMANS T, 2004. *Translation in Systems: Descriptive and System-oriented Approaches Explained* [M].Shanghai: Shanghai Foreign Language Education Press.

HABERMAS J, 2001.Objectivist and Subjectivist Approaches to Theory Formation in the Social Sciences[A]// *Pragmatics of Social Interaction*[C].The United States of America: Massachusetts Institute of Technology.

HALLIDAY M A K, HASAN R, 2001. *Cohesion in English*[M]. Beijing: Foreign Language Teaching and Research Press.

Toury G, 1995. *Descriptive Translation Studies and Beyond*[M].Amsterdam and Philadelphia: John Beniamins Publishing Company.

陈莉，2008. 汉语文学作品英译中的归化和异化问题：兼谈杨宪益在《儒林外史》中的文化翻译 [J]. 牡丹江大学学报（2）：99-101.

陈莉，2009. 近年《儒林外史》英译研究回眸 [J]. 时代文学（下半月）（4）：36-37.

丛倩倩，2011.《儒林外史》中带标记的被动句英译研究 [MA]. 大连：大连海事大学 .

丁水芳，丁建海，2013,《儒林外史》英译之杂合解读 [J]. 重庆交通大学学报（社会科学版）（2）：124-127.

段燕，2016, 身份视角下的称呼语翻译研究：以杨宪益英译《儒林外史》为例 [J]. 西华大学学报（哲学社会科学版）（5）：99-106.

冯洁，2016. 关联理论视域下《儒林外史》中习语的英译研究 [MA]. 成都：西南交通大学 .

傅敬民，2013. 全球结构视野下的翻译规范研究 [J]. 上海翻译（4）：11-15.

郭梦怡，2015. 阐释学视角下《儒林外史》两译本中译者主体性的对比研究 [MA]. 赣州：赣南师范学院 .

郭晓辉，2010. 论《儒林外史》中官职的英译 [MA]. 西安：西北大学 .

胡开宝，2015. 基于语料库的莎士比亚戏剧汉译研究 [M]. 上海：上海交通大学出版社 .

胡开宝，2011. 语料库翻译学概论 [M]. 上海：上海交通大学出版社 .

胡显耀，2006. 当代汉语翻译小说规范的语料库研究 [D]. 上海：华东师范大学 .

黄伯荣，廖序东，2014. 现代汉语（增订五版）下册 [M]. 北京：高等教育出版社 .

黄思怡，2015. 杨译《儒林外史》中描绘疯癫人物形象的语言翻译研究 [MA]. 衡阳：南华大学 .

刘瑜，2014. 范畴化视角下的汉英词汇范畴翻译研究 [MA]. 上海：华东理工大学 .

鲁迅，2009. 中国小说史略 [M]. 北京：北京大学出版社 .

潘慧兰，2008.《儒林外史》英译本中叙事语式的重建 [MA]. 长沙：中南大学 .

彭晓敏，2014. 顺应论视角下文化负载词的翻译研究 [MA]. 成都：成都理工大学 .

王映筠，2014. 汉语幽默文本英译研究 [MA]. 衡阳：南华大学 .

武光军，2014. 基于汉英类比语料库的翻译文本中的搭配特征研究 [M]. 北京：中国社会科学出版社 .

杨珉子，2012. 文化翻译理论视域下的汉语典籍英译 [MA]. 长沙：长沙理工大学 .

曾奇，2002.《儒林外史》英译本中文化词语的翻译 [MA]. 武汉：华中师范大学 .

朱思娟，2012. 从译者主体性看汉译英中的显与隐：杨宪益译《儒林外史》个案分析 [MA]. 长沙：中南大学 .

Appendix

The English Translation about Set Phrase in *The Scholars*

Type of Translation	Source Text	Translated Text	Frequency
normalized translation	1. 味同嚼蜡 2. 四散觅食 3. 擗踊哀号 4. 三年苫块 5. 龙凤之表 6. 飞黄腾达 7. 七手八脚 8. 时运不济 9. 花团锦簇 10. 獐头鼠目 11. 狗血喷头 12. 万贯家私 13. 连登黄甲 14. 含冤负屈 15. 釜底抽薪 16. 披麻戴孝 17. 一见如故 18. 暴躁如雷 19. 门墙桃李 20. 怒发冲冠 21. 退避三舍 22. 掌上之珠 23. 大吹大擂 24. 咂嘴弄舌 25. 举案齐眉	1.the taste is no better than chewed tallow 2.they were reduced to beggary 3.mourned and wept so bitterly 4.for three years he mourned 5.he looked every inch a king 6.passed the prefectural examination 7.lent a hand 8.unlucky 9.excellent 10.homely 11.poured out a torrent of abuse 12.pots of money 13.follow in rapid succession 14.underhand dealings 15.go to the root of the matter 16.wear heavy mourning 17.took to each other immediately 18.flew into a worse rage 19.his reputation 20.make your blood boil 21.none of us up to you 22.the apple of their eye 23.the musicians struck up 24.licking it up 25.husband and wife feasted together	50

Cont.

Type of Translation	Source Text	Translated Text	Frequency
normalized translation	26. 滚瓜烂熟 27. 九霄云外 28. 囹圄之中 29. 通财之义 30. 不胜叹息 31. 面如土色 32. 有名无实 33. 清秋大路 34. 素昧平生 35. 萍水相逢 36. 死也瞑目 37. 荣宗耀祖 38. 显亲扬名 39. 分庭抗礼 40. 手舞足蹈 41. 七横八竖 42. 螟蛉之子 43. 毛骨悚然 44. 挤眉弄眼 45. 怒气攻心 46. 坐吃山空 47. 喜从天降 48. 旦夕祸福 49. 自觉形秽 50. 面黄肌瘦	26.thoroughly mastered 27.forgotten all 28.died in prison 29.put their property at each other's disposal 30.could not repress a sigh of admiration 31.turned white 32.don't actually exist 33.close his case and see that he clears off 34.never had the honour of meeting 35.met by chance 36.die content 37.reflect credit upon your whole family 38.reflect credit on your family and to spread your fame 39.treated him as an equal 40.jumped for joy 41.falling to pieces 42.adopted son 43.sent chills up the two clerks' spines 44.winking and making signs to one another 45.choked with rage 46.ate their way through their silver 47.this was a stroke of luck 48.fortune is fickle 49.don't feel good enough for him 50.haggard,half-starved	50
foreign translation	1. 东张西望 2. 风餐露宿 3. 面黄肌瘦 4. 吟诗作画 5. 尖嘴猴腮 6. 打躬作别 7. 风卷残云 8. 丧家之狗 9. 漏网之鱼	1.looking right and left 2.braving the wind and dew 3.thin and sallow 4.chanting poetry, painting pictures 5.your mouth sticks out and you've a chin like an ape's 6.bowed and parted 7.a whirlwind scattering wisps of cloud 8.as stray dogs 9.as fish escaping from the net	

Cont.

Type of Translation	Source Text	Translated Text	Frequency
foreign translation	10. 如雷灌耳 11. 缎靴金带 12. 晓行夜宿 13. 牙关咬紧 14. 万家烟火 15. 同生同死 16. 挥金如土 17. 蓬蒿满径 18. 骨瘦如柴 19. 张灯结彩 20. 揖让升阶 21. 如梦方醒 22. 尊卑长幼 23. 聒耳得紧	10.resounds like thunder 11.satin shoes and gold belt 12.travelling by day and resting by night 13.clenched her teeth 14.the smoke from the thousands of houses 15.live and die with such a man 16.scatter gold about like dirt 17.the yard with weeds 18.he was nothing but skin and bones 19.hung with lanterns and decorated with streamers 20.bowing as he invited them to ascend the steps 21.coming out of darkness into the bright light of day 22.young folk must obey their elders 23.it jars on my ears	23
ellipsis	1. 如狼似虎 2. 光天化日 3. 忍气吞声		3